My friends Amanda and Anne-Renee de[...] face as moms to be present with our fa[...] in a million different directions. The pra[...] *Shiny Things* will meet you right where you are while pointing you back to the moment-by-moment help offered to us by Jesus Himself. Such a needed message for us moms today.

Lysa TerKeurst, *New York Times* bestselling author and president of
Proverbs 31 Ministries

This is a kind book for any mom who feels pushed around by her schedule and pulled away by distraction. What Amanda and Anne-Renee do for moms in *Shiny Things* is to bring us back to center by reminding us of our most basic loves—home, good work, family, dear friends, and a God who holds us all together. I'm grateful for the friendship they have with each other that they graciously extend to us in the pages of this book.

Emily P. Freeman, *Wall Street Journal* bestselling author of *Simply Tuesday*
and host of *The Next Right Thing* podcast

Amanda and Anne-Renee remind us that moms are not robots—we have real demands on our time and space, but also some very real limitations. *Shiny Things* is an excellent read that helps us see how choosing wisely, with the bigger picture always in mind, is key. This book is like sitting with two friends who help me focus on my relationship with God, my priority people, and my God-given role as a mom.

Nicki Koziarz, bestselling author and speaker

There are a thousand inconsequential distractions every day that try to get in the way of God's priorities for my work and my everyday life. This book will help you keep your eyes fixed on the work and the people God wants you to serve and to love.

Jennifer Dukes Lee, author of *It's All Under Control*

Anne-Renee and Amanda have written a beautiful message to moms, reminding us all about what is truly significant about our role in our families and the purpose God has for us, right where we are!

Jennifer Smith, author of *The Unveiled Wife* and *Wife After God*

I don't know of a single mom who isn't tempted by distraction. *Shiny Things* is what we've needed—a gracious guide to help us live and love according to our actual priorities instead of getting sidetracked by the shiny substitutes all around us. In this practical and personal book, Anne-Renee and Amanda offer us an opportunity to reassess our values, refocus our hearts, and recapture our time…all so we can honor and steward our unique calling as mothers.

Leeana Tankersley, author of *Begin Again*

This book is your survival guide to the stop-go-stop-go rollercoaster of parenting. It's not another *to-do*. It's a *to-don't*. Here's your permission slip to stop what's sucking the life out of you and find new ways to focus on what's life-giving to you and your family.

Lisa-Jo Baker, bestselling author of *Never Unfriended* and cohost of the *Out of the Ordinary* podcast

For all of us moms who have felt the weight of discouragement and distraction, Anne-Renee and Amanda are a welcome voice of reassurance and hope. *Shiny Things* is their gentle but genuine reminder we need to let go of our guilt and self-imposed expectations and rest in the grace we have in Christ.

Teri Lynne Underwood, author of *Praying for Girls*

If all the people and projects that naturally come with the role of "mom" have you pulled in umpteen directions, this book is for you. *Shiny Things* will help you to strategically sort through all that is vying for your attention and set your sights on what really counts. Amanda and Anne-Renee have created a practical resource that will empower moms to fulfill their high and holy calling without losing their focus—or their minds!

Karen Ehman, Proverbs 31 Ministries speaker and *New York Times* bestselling author of *Keep It Shut*

The difficult work of motherhood has often caught me by surprise. How could something so good be so hard? With heartfelt transparency, Amanda and Anne-Renee bring clarity to our calling and give us the perspective we need to move forward with hope and confidence.

Ruth Schwenk, author of *Pressing Pause* and *The Better Mom*

AMANDA BACON and
ANNE-RENEE GUMLEY

HARVEST HOUSE PUBLISHERS
EUGENE, OREGON

Cover by Faceout Studio

Published in association with The Fedd Agency, Inc., PO Box 341973, Austin, TX 78734.

Shiny Things

Copyright © 2019 Amanda Bacon and Anne-Renee Gumley
Published by Harvest House Publishers
Eugene, Oregon 97408
www.harvesthousepublishers.com

ISBN 978-0-7369-7367-0 (pbk.)
ISBN 978-0-7369-7368-7 (eBook)

Library of Congress Cataloging-in-Publication Data is on file at the Library of Congress, Washington, DC.

Printed in the United States of America

19 20 21 22 23 24 25 26 27 / BP-GL / 10 9 8 7 6 5 4 3 2 1

To mothers everywhere—
because training up young humans in the way they should go
is hard and holy work.

Contents

Introduction

Amanda and Anne-Renee

The rising sun's rays crept around the edges of the curtains much earlier than she preferred. *At least the sun is shining,* she thought. The recent string of gray days had left her feeling a bit down. For some reason, she couldn't shake the cloud of dissatisfaction that seemed to be hanging over her head.

Trying to pinpoint the exact source of her angst, she started making a mental list of the items that brought her life throughout the day and those that were bringing her low. It didn't take long. A lot of activities brought her life. She loved her kids and spending quality time pouring into them. She adored those moments when she really engaged with her whole self. She loved God with everything in her and having creative outlets, a job, volunteer work, and relationships that fed her soul.

She also enjoyed the ability to be in constant contact with the world through her phone, and she spent a good amount of time with her computer. Being on her laptop made her feel like she was accomplishing something, even if she was just reading an article.

These things gave her life, but she often felt conflicted about how she spent her time. *What and whom should get the best of her? Why did it seem more enticing to choose lesser things over lasting things? And what qualified as lesser?*

She continued to ponder these early morning thoughts as she swung her feet to the floor and then quietly padded to the kitchen. A glorious whiff of fresh coffee greeted her senses, and she was thankful she'd programmed the coffeemaker to do its thing the night before. Maybe it wasn't the best idea to stay up late watching another episode of that TV show everyone was talking about.

Pouring a generous amount of coffee into her favorite floral mug, she breathed in its caffeinated goodness. It took all her willpower to ignore the new magazine beckoning her from the end of the kitchen counter. She walked past it resolutely, promising herself that she wouldn't peek until she'd spent at least a few minutes in the Word.

The house was miraculously quiet as she ambled toward the living room. She couldn't believe the kids hadn't come looking for her yet. Her favorite chair waited for her by the window, and she sank into its cushion, holding her steaming cup of courage. She reached for her Bible and let out a deep breath, the one she'd been holding all week, it seemed.

Moments after settling into her reading, she heard a ding from her phone. She wondered if it was an important ding, or just an ordinary ding. Then she heard a louder noise that sounded like it was coming from a human, but she wasn't sure. Maybe it was just the cat, or so she hoped.

The next sound was indeed human, coming from the two youngest in the family. One walked down the stairs to greet the day with a furrowed brow and grumpy disposition, and the other was somehow ravenous, as if he hadn't had a meal in days. She set aside her coffee and Bible with an audible sigh and welcomed them onto her lap for a quick hug.

The day had begun, and the time she'd spent alone equaled less than five minutes. She wished her children had given her more time. A few minutes alone in the morning wasn't too much to ask, was it?

Then it hit her—she knew exactly why she'd been off recently. Or maybe it was more than just recently. Maybe it had been years. She wasn't sure. She just knew something had to change.

She had been fighting the constant pull to do what she wanted, when she wanted. She was struggling to keep her top priorities in the top spot. Some days she didn't even know how to tell what her highest priority should be.

She was distracted…and conflicted. One second she'd wanted to bark at her kids to march back upstairs until she was ready to see them, and the very next second she'd wanted to pull them close, look into their eyes, and will time to stand still as she memorized everything about them.

Like an invisible bag of bricks, all that distraction and conflict was weighing her down.

Ah, yes—this is the dilemma all moms face. We know exactly how she feels, don't we? So pulled. So overwhelmed. So desperate for a moment of peace and quiet.

This is the reality we, too, struggle with—all day, every day. The mom in this story is us; we are her. We understand the desire to love our families well, but to also engage in other activities we enjoy. We have felt the magnetic pull to steer away from what's truly important and focus on what feels different and looks shiny. Yes, we want to love God and our families, but the idea of slipping into the pool of distraction right in front of us and floating in it for a while is just so enticing!

We have yet to meet a mom with no connection to distraction.

We also had no idea how easy it would be to become distracted while writing about the concept of distraction. How our minds and fingers would twitch to do something else as we tried to sit still to write about a focused life. How our minds would long to escape to other places, the exotic or even the ordinary and mundane—anywhere, as long as it was somewhere else.

We all struggle to stay focused and not fall victim to distraction. And disruption in the life of a mom often comes without invitation or beckoning. All it takes is a phone call, one child hollering *"Mooooooom,"* an e-mail reminder about a big online sale, a text from a friend, or one ding from our phone telling us we have an unread message, and we're off, running the race of the distracted mom. Maybe your distractions, your shiny things, don't require cords or batteries. Maybe for you it's puzzles, DIY projects, painting, shopping, knitting, daydreaming, organizing, watering your plants, a new library book, or even cleaning.

We wish we could say we're more distracted by housework than technology, but we're not. The desire to see what's going on in the world and communicate (hello, extroverts) is strong, so our phones are probably the most powerful distraction we face in our days. Maybe for you the distraction is your stressful job or the stress of a life crisis. If so, we're so sorry. We've been where you are. Stress does a number on our mothering, but there's still hope. We just might have to work a little more diligently to stay the course.

Our stories may look different from yours. That's completely fine; we can still be friends. Different is our specialty. But at the core, most moms have the same goal: to live and love well.

The two of us are what we like to call the Mom-Opposites.

Anne-Renee has two kids. Amanda has eight.

Anne-Renee works outside the home at her family's party and event supply company. Amanda is a stay-at-home mom who works for Proverbs 31 Ministries, spending one day in the office and completing the rest of her work at home. Anne-Renee's kids are in public school. Half of Amanda's kids are homeschooled, and the other half are in public school.

And now, to make the opposite nature of our friendship even more dramatic, we live on opposite sides of the country after living 15 minutes down the road from each other for more than a decade. Anne-Renee lives in Alaska, and Amanda lives in North Carolina.

Despite our differences, we've been dear friends for 14 years. We love the dynamic of our differing lives; it's never been in the way. Our differences have only caused us to be more compassionate and understanding of each other and of moms who live differently than we do. Though our lives look poles apart from the outside, they have plenty of similarities.

For starters, we're both nuts about our kids, and we want them to be our top priority after God and our husbands. We don't want to throw away the years we have with our children, pursuing temporary pleasures and chasing worthless desires. We'd like to be known as intentional, steady, focused, purposeful, loving, and engaged.

We want all these good things, but we're both majorly prone to distraction.

Don't think of us as "experts" writing a book to help the masses who haven't yet figured everything out. No. *Please, no.* We don't have this down; that's why we're writing this book. We need this message, and we want change in our lives so much that we're willing to bare our souls and help carve a path we can all walk down together toward victory over distractedness. How about considering us your trusty guides instead?

Because we know you're busy and your time is valuable, we've arranged each of the ten sections in this book into four short chapters, each an easy-peasy five- to ten-minute read. They're perfect for the carpool line, doctor's office, naptime, early morning, while nursing, or when taking a quick trip to the bathroom. (We've heard from various secret sources that the most effective method for reading in there is to lock the door and ignore any wiggling fingers underneath it.)

We also want to give you a heads-up that of the four chapters in each part, the first two are written by Amanda and the last two are written by Anne-Renee. That's our pattern throughout the entire book.

At the end of each section, you'll find a handy place where we've listed key points we'd like you to remember, provided scriptures for you to hold on to, and given you one or two challenges to consider. This is our version of a cheat sheet—something you can flip to for reminders whenever you need them. We truly want this walk toward living undistracted to be feasible, easy to follow, and fulfilling.

The pull to set aside our favorite people or the work God has set before us for something shiny is magnetic. Daily monotony and the challenging work we mothers do every single day often causes us to desire something soothing and satisfying, something that feels easier in the moment instead of what's going to be good in the long term. This is our dilemma.

The pull to set aside our favorite people or the work God has set before us for something shiny is magnetic.

Won't you walk with us as we set off on a path toward an undistracted life? One where Jesus is King and everything else falls into its proper place as we seek His kingdom first in our families, and then in everything else we're made stewards of for our time here on earth.

As we're learning to live on purpose in a world of distractions, let's begin with giving all the craziness to the only One who can handle our mayhem, struggles, and tears. We desperately need His help and for Him to guide and instruct our ways, all for His glory.

A Prayer as We Begin

Father, we love You. We want to honor You above all else. Thank You for making us mothers. Thank You for trusting us with our children—what gifts they are! We come before You, hands open, asking You to be our help and strength as we seek to be moms who are undistracted. May we bring You glory as we walk toward living a focused and intentional life for Your kingdom's sake. In Jesus's name, amen.

Part One

The Pull

1

Don't Blame It on the Shiny Things

Amanda

All that glitters is not gold.
WILLIAM SHAKESPEARE[1]

I stood outside our double-wide trailer, wearing my homemade turquoise leggings complete with stirrups. They were shimmery, fabulous, and all I ever wanted to wear.

I was seven years old, and I thought I was the absolute coolest as I strutted to the front of the garage where the bug zapper swung from a hook. I'd park myself there, watching bug after unsuspecting bug fall to its doom with a hiss and sizzle. I shook my head in amazement that bugs would allow themselves to be lured by the light. Didn't they know they'd be zapped? Hadn't the warning to steer clear of the glow been passed down through the insect generations?

Insects are so attracted to light that nothing can save them once they're pulled in that direction. They're like magnets to refrigerators, little kids to dirt, and moms to their phones.

We're being pulled too. Pulled by anything and everything that feels enjoyable in the moment. We don't want to miss out on and ignore the most important people and responsibilities in our lives, but the draw to do something other than what is needed right now is strong.

May I tell you something you absolutely already know? It's because real-life mothering is sometimes mundane.

Even though we love being moms and we love our kids, we still must walk through experiences and do things day in and day out that aren't necessarily fun. Real-life mothering calls for responsibility, intentionality, and a whole lot of sacrifice, a life most definitely not all rainbows and big bouquets of daisies.

While sitting in a coffee shop recently, I overheard a new mom talking to a friend she hadn't seen since she'd had her baby. When her friend asked how everything was going, she said, "No one ever told me how hard it really is."

I wanted to buy that girl a venti white chocolate mocha with whip, look her square in the eyes, and tell her she's doing a lovely job with her daughter. I also wanted to tell her she's right—it's hard—yet mothering is a worthwhile endeavor that will bring the biggest blessings into her life, some obvious, some not so obvious. No one ever told her how hard motherhood is, but maybe no one's ever told her how glorious it can be.

Motherhood presents a unique dichotomy, where the loveliest of lovelies live alongside the challenge that naturally exists when we're engaged in anything worthwhile. Months or years that feel like centuries, filled with lack of sleep, illness, behavioral issues, relational difficulties, and daily sameness, wear on us. And no one is immune to boredom with mundane routines or wanting to avoid what they dislike.

Some days, all I want to do is act like a three-year-old—stamp my foot, cross my arms, stick out a pouty bottom lip, howl at the too-hard circumstances before me, and run away to Target. Just because motherhood sometimes lacks ease and pleasure doesn't mean it's not also good and beautiful. We just might need to grow to fully appreciate its beauty.

Growth comes from walking with God through the toughest of circumstances. We like growth in theory; it's the good part we all want. The process of getting there is what's unpopular. I don't think I've ever heard someone say, "Oh, I learned so much about God and myself when the seas of my life were smooth. Having no wants or cares grew me in ways I'd never imagined." Uh, no. We like smooth seas because they're comfortable and temporarily easier, but they don't do a whole lot to form our character.

English theologian Leslie Weatherhead once explained,

> Like all men I love and prefer the sunny uplands of experience, where health, happiness, and success abound, but I have learned far more about God, life, and myself in the darkness of fear and failure than I have ever learned in the sunshine. There are such things as the treasures of the darkness. The darkness, thank God, passes. But what one learns in the darkness one possesses forever.[2]

We're familiar with feelings of fear and failure, sometimes in the same thought. But we're also familiar with those treasures tucked in between the hard stretches. Those are the good and lovely parts. The moments we promise we'll remember forever. The growth we see in ourselves and our kids. The beautiful life we've been given even when the way seems cloudy—or murky with half a box of Cheerios floating in it, depending on the mom stage you're in.

Beauty is always present, even when we can't see how or where. There will always be beauty, because there will always be God. There will always be hard stuff to do or walk through and distractions to avoid, along with a whole lot of need to refocus. Some parenting moments will bring us to our knees, and in some seasons we'll fear we might not survive. But there will always be God. *Always.*

Beauty is always present, even whe
we can't see how or where.

The dilemma is that the challenges of motherhood warrant so much of our thoughts and attention that they can overshadow the beauty. We're bored. We're tired. We're questioning. And drowning the difficult parts of our lives with momentary pleasure becomes easier in the moment.

Sometimes we just don't feel like making lunches or cleaning toilets, so we start pinning Pinterest recipes for birthday cakes we'll never make or instructions for Christmas ornaments made with safety pins. So yes, real life can be hard, hard, hard, but sometimes we're overcome by the "just don't wannas."

Sometimes I don't feel like playing cars with my youngest guy or listening to my teenage sons give the play-by-play of the movie they watched at a youth group event. It's not because I'm unloving or uninterested in my kids' lives, but because I'm 100 percent human. So are you. We aren't robots, so it isn't physically, mentally, or emotionally possible to do all things well, all the time. Perfection isn't required; it's the deep conviction and decision of our hearts turned Godward that counts.

Everyday life tends to ask some tricky things of us, and sometimes it asks some tough questions too, like *What's most important to you?* So much vies for our attention, but what are our priorities? We decide what our priorities are every single day, usually without much forethought or prior planning. Sometimes we choose wisely, and sometimes we don't. We're distractible, so easily allowing ourselves to stray off track.

We want to be undistracted moms who have clear priorities and direction, choosing to spend our hours on what's meaningful—our relationship with God and growing in Him, pursuing the work He's put before us and engaging with our families. Not only are we asked to name what's most important to us, but life begs the question, *How will you honor and care for these important things?*

This is the question we'll try to answer together. How will we honor and care for the things and people most important to us? How will we honor and care for everything God has given us and asked us to steward?

If we recognize what's most important to us, why is staying focused on it so hard? We could easily blame it on our modern culture with its flashing lights, dinging phones, and shiny devices that invite us to more pleasure and fewer doldrums, more escapes and fewer prisons (real or perceived). But technology or not, the truth is the pull has always been there.

I recently read an amusing story about Abraham Lincoln. When his four sons were small, he would pull them up and down the street in a wagon with one hand and hold the book he was reading in the other. Occasionally, one of his little guys would topple out and be left behind by his father, who was completely engrossed in his book and didn't hear him cry. Not until onlookers notified him of the debacle would he circle back to gather his son.[3]

Fast-forward to our mothers' day and age. The moms of their generation could be distracted by things like television, books, and movies; phone calls to and from friends; volunteer opportunities and work; hobbies; and even perfectionism. Don't forget, though, that they also had all sorts of new technology arriving on the scene. Think cordless telephones replacing phones with curly cords attached to the wall, desktop computers, and eventually those mobile phones that took two hands to hold.

Shiny things have always existed. Though these inventions from days gone by don't sound all that exciting to us now, each generation is exposed to bright new forms of distraction.

We could claim all day long that the many choices presented to us in this modern age are at the root of our distractedness, but truly, every generation has had its fair share of distractions. The number of choices we're presented with today just makes it easier for us to move in the direction we might later regret, easier to succumb to distraction.

How can we avoid this pull and make choices we'll be proud of later? Let's talk about it.

2

What It Costs

Amanda

There will come a day when she no longer wants to hold my hand.
So I will hold it while I still can.

Rachel Macy Stafford[1]

What we decide to let distract us is a true indicator of what we unwittingly make important without first calculating the cost.

When we reach for the newest bestseller at every opportunity rather than God's Word, there's a cost. When we choose to mindlessly scroll through our Facebook newsfeed instead of engaging with our children, there's a cost. When we spend an unhealthy amount of time looking at how everyone else is doing life instead of just doing our own life, there's a cost. When we compare our kids to hers instead of appreciating the God-given uniqueness in our own children, there's a cost. When we're distracted by worry and all the what-ifs rather than trusting our lives into our loving Father's hands, there's a cost.

Distraction comes with costs we don't often stop to think about, because, well, we're too distracted. Most times, we don't even realize how distracted we've allowed ourselves to be. The pushing aside of what's most sacred to us in favor of easy escapes is a big deal, but it's never too late to lay claim to what we deem most valuable.

Now is a good time.

I'm sure you, just as Anne-Renee and I do, desire to be an undivided, focused, faithful, and dependable mom. We long for our first priorities to be our first priority. Naming our priorities isn't usually too hard for us. If you're a fan of list-making like me, you dig hashing them out, because, obviously, that involves making a list. (I'm convinced list-making is one of my love languages. I'd happily make a list about absolutely nothing if you asked me to. Amen.)

Naming and listing what's most dear to us is the easy part. Living with our priorities consistently in that order is the problem. The good and bad news about priorities is they only get out of line if we move them.

The good and bad news about priorities is they only get out of line if we move them.

Jesus spoke about priorities in the Bible on several accounts. Promise me you won't glaze over here, but the one that strikes me most is about Mary of Bethany sitting and listening to Jesus rather than scurrying around the house with her sister, Martha, who was in a tizzy because the Lord had come to visit their home. Luke 10:38-42 tells the story like this:

> Now as they went on their way, Jesus entered a village. And a woman named Martha welcomed him into her house. And she had a sister called Mary, who sat at the Lord's feet and listened to his teaching. But Martha was distracted with much serving. And she went up to him and said, "Lord, do you not care that my sister has left me to serve alone? Tell her then to help me." But the Lord answered her, "Martha, Martha, you are anxious and troubled about many things, but one thing is necessary. Mary has chosen the good portion, which will not be taken away from her."

I don't know if it's that Mary and Martha are women or that I can relate to each of them in a different way, but I'm drawn into their situation. Like Martha, I can be distracted and harried, full of expectations for everyone around me. After all, she was hosting the Lord! I mean, who else was going to prepare the food and get the house ready? That seems like a good reason for her to be a little edgy, especially if she was a perfectionist hoping to make a good impression.

On the flip side, I can be focused and worshipful, sitting with Jesus like Mary did. I imagine I wouldn't want to leave His side for a second if we were in the same house.

When we read this, it's obvious who's making the better choice, but that's after we've read Jesus's response to Martha and let it soak in. We've been Martha more times than we'd like to admit.

This story, only five verses long, has been illustrated countless times for countless audiences, so I'm just going to point out a simple truth we gain from this passage: *Mary had her priorities in order.*

It probably wouldn't have been wrong for her to jump up and help her sister, but her priority was Jesus, so she fought to keep Him in the top spot. I admire her singular vision here. No amount of pressure or guilt from her sister would sway her from following through with what was best.

Imagine how our worlds would change if we were this focused on keeping the important stuff of life consistently at the top of our lists? If there were no question as to where our loyalties lie? God, along with our most important people and callings, would get the best of us, and whatever lay at the bottom would get the leftovers, instead of the other way around.

3

A Million Different Directions

Anne-Renee

A good laugh and a long sleep are the two best cures for anything.

IRISH PROVERB

Some stories your children just won't let you live down. Like that one time I attempted to make pancakes out of hummus dip.

It was early. Way too early, and Mama hadn't had her cup of coffee yet. I was stumbling around the kitchen in a sleepy daze, doing my best to oversee the last bits of school lunch assembly, check work e-mails on my phone, and make breakfast. I grabbed a heavy glass container out of the fridge, thinking it was the leftover pancake mix I had whipped up the previous morning.

No sooner had I placed a perfect little mound of batter in the hot pan than I realized my mistake. A pungent odor hit our noses and awakened our senses like none other. Not the sweet smell of frying flapjacks, mind you, but a potent, knock-you-down kind of aroma—the unmistakable smell of fried garlic. Clearly this was not the pancake batter from yesterday's breakfast, but the garlic hummus from last night's dinner.

The kids were dying—on the floor laughing like a bunch of hyenas.

Their eyes stung with the hilarity of the moment and the overwhelming stench of burned garlic. Our kitchen reeked for days.

This story has been told and retold by my kids. Every time it's recalled, I can't help but think, *Why couldn't I focus on just one thing that morning? Why was I trying to do three things at once?* I know the answer: I was tired. I was distracted. On their own, those two things are dangerous, but put them together, and boy oh boy, they're deadly.

It seems so hard to focus these days, and focusing on only one thing at a time seems almost impossible.

As busy moms, we're the worker bees in our homes as well as the project managers. We are the brains *and* the hands. We don't just oversee and delegate; we're the ones who make it happen. Most of the planning, scheduling, shopping, and remembering of facts (birthdays, appointments, school project deadlines, whether the bathroom has toilet paper) falls on our mothering shoulders. It's no wonder we struggle to relax well in our own homes. The mother load is always there. Waiting. Beckoning. Deterring us from mental freedom.

I could chalk it all up to the busyness of my season. This whole mixing motherhood, work, and ministry act is hectic at best. My days seem to melt into one another in a drippy mess of to-dos and partially checked-off boxes. Frankly, it's exhausting trying so hard to do something—*anything*—well, yet feeling defeated at the end of the day, as though I've accomplished nothing.

I know I'm not alone in this. So many responsibilities seem to be pulling at us these days. The first, and probably the most obvious responsibilities are the visible needs of our children, from the early years on. The feeding. The burping. The diaper changing. More feeding. The cleanup—oh, the constant cleanup! The tending. The tidying. The rallying. The reminding. The driving. A never-ending cycle of needs.

All good things, but tiring things. And when we're pulled in a million different directions, too, it's easy to lose track of what's important.

Is it just the daily to-dos that keep us from focusing on the imperative, though? Or is it possibly something more?

When we're pulled in a million different directions, it's easy to lose track of what's important.

Just like yesterday's mother, today's mom is bombarded from morning 'til night with outside voices trying to get inside her head. They try to speak over the murmuring of her heart, the deep yearning of calling, and the promptings of the Holy Spirit. The voices are the same, but the clothing they wear has changed through the generations.

Social media. E-mail. Text messaging. Video chats. TV. Movies at your fingertips. All those voices feed our insatiable desire to see what everyone else is doing, from celebrities to friends to frenemies. Think gorgeous kitchens, breathtaking scenery, sparkling sequins, pulsating lights, and loud music all rolled into one. These flickers of disruption halt our course and attempt to alter the outcome of our day, not to mention the effect they have on our attitude and overall desire to serve our families and those God puts in our path.

Anyone who's had poor cell phone connection on a trip knows what I'm talking about. When the magnetic pull is missing, we feel at a loss. We have no games to play, no way to search for instant answers to questions, no way to see what everyone else in the world is doing and eating and experiencing.

Our hands and minds itch to check our feeds rather than feed our families. I mean, really. Providing meals day in and day out? Why are our people never satisfied? Why can't we feed them once and be done? Hungry bellies and children begging for our attention. It's never ending.

But don't you worry. We're not saying all technology, social media, and screened entertainment is bad. No need to cover up your phone with the cushion next to you or run outside and bury your TV's remote control. It would be so easy for us to point a finger at all the gadgets and gizmos and say the reason we can't focus is all the noise.

No, to be fair and weigh both sides, we must look at the good along with the bad. And we do have a choice, you know.

The digital age has also provided all sorts of new platforms to proclaim God's truth. Think of all the online Bible studies, podcasts, satellite conferences, webcasts, and sermons you've listened to or watched in the last year. Thanks to developing audio and visual technology, we have new mediums to further the kingdom. These powerful tools allow us to speak truth and deliver God's Word in ways we couldn't without such a framework. They've opened so many doors, bonding and knitting hearts from all across the globe to be beacons of light in dark places we never dreamed we would trod.

But like any flashing light, the digital age can also be distracting. In the words of Oscar Wilde,

> To drift with every passion till my soul
> Is a stringed lute on which all winds can play,
> Is it for this that I have given away
> Mine ancient wisdom, and austere control?[1]

What controls our mind controls our schedule, and what controls our schedule shapes our future. Bottom line: A little bit in moderation is better for the hungry soul than consuming the whole orchard. So why not save ourselves the bellyache?

What controls our mind controls our schedule, and what controls our schedule shapes our future.

Pile together all the to-dos and extra voices, and then add a dose of your own personality into the mix: The procrastinator (who likes to put off the difficult), the project junkie (who loves to start but hates to finish—not mentioning any names), the discontent wife (who has a desire for the different). The guilt-ridden, the fear-driven, the worry-wart, or the mom who'd rather jump onto Facebook than clean the faces of her children. Add all these together and you have a magnificent mixed cocktail of crazy called the Distracted Mom.

**We want to be focused, but we must fight
to stay fixed on the significant.**

We want to be focused, but we must fight to stay fixed on the significant. We are the sidetracked. The preoccupied. The confused. The conflicted. The dreamy. The inattentive. The obsessed. The bored. We have been known to abandon our assigned posts from time to time in hot pursuit of other things. Because we don't want to miss out. We're curious. We want to know more and see more.

We're fueled by various vices we allow to have power over us. Our hearts and our minds feel like taffy, stretched and strained beyond capacity. We're struggling to keep our eyes on the prize. But we want to. We do.

If it weren't for all those shiny things that pull us away.

4

What If

Anne-Renee

*Dance like no one is watching. Because they're
not. They're checking their phones.*

Anonymous

I stare at the blades of grass dancing in the breeze just beyond my picnic blanket. A boisterous seagull calls out as he returns to his leftover Taco Bell lunch hidden under a nearby bench. He happily sings a noisy duet with a faraway train. The train chugging out its own solo as it gets closer and closer to the park.

I glance at my Bible study book, wondering what is wrong with my brain that I can't concentrate for a ten-minute segment of time. But the grass, the seagull, and the train have momentarily captured my attention. I am a prisoner to my surroundings, captive to my own imaginings.

Then I do what many a mom with a glorious two-hour break would do. I grab my phone and start flipping aimlessly through my Instagram feed, suddenly oh so incredibly interested in what everyone else on the planet is doing and saying. For 20 minutes straight, I'm sucked into the social media vortex! Guilt begins to seep in, causing me to shake my head and sigh. But I continue, giving my consent, allowing my mind and fingers to be magnetized to the device.

Meanwhile, my Bible study book sits on my lap completely unread, and the takeaway section at the end of the chapter is once more left blank.

Distraction strikes yet again.

Wouldn't it be nice if we could live in a world completely free of distraction? Just for a moment, close your eyes and imagine with me how different life would be.

Are you envisioning an isolated beach somewhere? Perhaps a private cabin in the woods. A deserted island. Or a quiet spa with no one under the age of 21.

Sounds heavenly, right?

But alas, it will never be. (Sad, I know.)

I wish I could promise you 100 percent that if you did a certain number of things you could be rid of distraction forever. But I'd be lying if I tried to sell you that guarantee.

Something will *always* pop up, begging for our attention like an annoying jack-in-the-box that bursts forth whenever it wants. Good things. Hard things. Amusing things. Destructive things.

Amanda and I can't promise you'll never battle distraction again, because being distracted isn't merely a habit to kick or a disease to cure. Truthfully, you may fight distraction until the day you die.

One thing you'll not hear from us in this book is a set list of how-tos, to-dos, or The ABCs of the Undistracted Life. (And all the tired mamas said *Amen!* because, gracious, who needs another list of rules to follow?)

Recognizing we're distracted women, however, helps put us back in the driver's seat of doing something about it, facing it head-on and admitting we're a preoccupied people in need of a Savior. Oh, how we need Him!

We need Him to push us toward the good things, the eternal things, the things that matter most. To help shift our focus from ourselves to where it needs to be—on Him.

We want to be intentional people, women of purpose with eyes fixed and faith firm.

Let's join in this journey toward being undistracted, united by the desire to pursue what truly matters: our faith, our families, and the people God puts in our path.

While we're getting it all out there on the table, let's also acknowledge it might be difficult. Facing distraction will require some discipline, and to some, discipline can seem like a dirty word.

We get it. We do. It's hard to stay on track. It's uncomfortable, and downright boring at times. I don't know about you, but I'm also not very keen on saying no to myself (I say as I nibble on a Reese's Peanut Butter Cup while composing this confession). Saying no means employing self-control, and control over one's self, thoughts, and actions is hard. Very hard indeed.

But not impossible.

Let's look at where we are. We know we're being pulled—daily, hourly, minute by minute—and we realize what's doing some of the pulling. It's all those things that pile up and pull at us, calling us away from the important, keeping us from good mothering, from mothering the way God intended.

But it's the doing something about it that rankles the senses.

Distraction can be a barometer of sorts, an indicator of what's truly important in our lives.

Distraction can be a barometer of sorts, an indicator of what's truly important in our lives. We don't like to hear that. Not one bit. We want to be good moms. We want our children to rise and called us blessed, and for all the angels to sing *Glory hallelujah*.

But it seems rather hard to do when all these distractions keep popping up and getting in the way, grabbing at our sense of concentration, waving their flags to capture our hearts and our attention.

Enough, we say.

Yes, this quest might get a little sticky, a little uncomfortable. But it's gonna be good. We promise. We're in this together as women who desire to pursue God and His best. Let's move to love our people well and work to leave a legacy of unshakeable faith for our families and beyond.

Maybe the next time I'm basking in God's creation, marveling at His works, my awe of what's going on around me and my burgeoning wonder at who He is will propel me right back into studying and soaking up His Word. Maybe. Just maybe.

All the Good Things

The Pull

To Remember

- Just because motherhood sometimes lacks ease and pleasure doesn't mean it's not also good and beautiful.
- Growth comes from walking with God through the toughest of circumstances.
- Beauty is always present, even when we can't see how or where.
- Perfection isn't required; the deep conviction and decision of our hearts turned Godward is what counts.
- The good and bad news about priorities is they only get out of line if we move them.
- When we're pulled in a million different directions, it's easy to lose track of what's important.

To Hold On To

You keep him in perfect peace whose mind is stayed on you, because he trusts in you. Trust in the LORD forever, for the LORD God is an everlasting rock (Isaiah 26:3-4).

You will seek me and find me, when you seek me with all your heart (Jeremiah 29:13).

To Consider

- Name two shiny things that are pulling you toward distraction.
- What can you do this week to focus on the needs in front of you instead of what's pulling you?

Part Two

Right Things, Wrong Times

5

Rescuing Our Own Lives

Amanda

When the Well's dry, they know the Worth of Water.
BENJAMIN FRANKLIN[1]

Today I'm home alone, a nearly impossible feat considering nine other people are in my immediate family. I can count on one hand how many times I've been alone in my own home in the last year. Make that two fingers. I can count the occurrences on two fingers.

Life has been intensely pressing with several house-to-house transitions, a cross-country move, new schools, a new church, job searching, new jobs, a relational crisis, missing everything familiar, and keeping our family afloat through it all.

My husband, Jeremy, is giving me some time to breathe for the afternoon. He's seen the burden in my eyes. You know, that sort of burden you just keep carrying around because you don't know how not to? It's the kind of burden that feels like lead is hanging around your shoulders and too many tabs are open on the computer of your mind. Yes, that kind.

The circles under my eyes are dark, everything feels laborious, and my brain is absolutely fried. I desperately need a breather or an entire week of sleep, but there doesn't seem to be any way for that to happen anytime soon, if ever.

My life needs a rescue. I'm guessing yours does too. So desperately.

An afternoon of rest is a start and a huge help toward relieving the immediate pressure, but it's not a fix. We need a rescue, but how? Is it possible for the pace of life as we know it to change?

To clarify, I'm not talking about salvation or somehow saving ourselves from hardship. I'm talking about the way we're living our lives. The way we work and serve and give until we're practically a shell of a person. How we rescue and resuscitate every living thing except ourselves.

We rescue and resuscitate every living thing except ourselves.

My whole soul exhales to avoid tensing as I remember that shell. I've been that shell of a woman at several points as a mom, and I don't wish to go back there—ever. I remember them too well—those seasons of on-the-floor-leftover-me.

If you've been there, too, you know it's at that point we're sure we're of no more substance than the translucent skin a shedding reptile leaves before slinking away, leaving its lifeless leftovers behind.

Before I go on, I need to tell you I'm vehemently opposed to all things slithery, and I probably shoved my fingers in my ears and *la-la-la'd* my way through seventh grade science class when they got to this part. Ask me how I like living in the snake-infested state of North Carolina after living in snake-less Alaska for 30 years.

Anyway, if you're anti-snake like me, you're probably not eager for more information on these reptiles to take up space in your brain, but stay with me. A snake's skin doesn't grow like human skin does, so a time comes when the outer layer is so tight and so unhealthy that the snake must shed it. This process is called *ecdysis*. Ecdysis is necessary for the snake to continue growing, and it also leaves behind any parasites that might have attached themselves to the snake.

That squeezing sensation tells the snake something important: *It's time to cast off something.*

Maybe the shell-on-the-floor version of ourselves isn't such a bad thing. Maybe it's an important indicator that we fly right by if we're not paying attention. When we get to that point, perhaps we need to be more intentional about really looking at our lives.

That squeeze needs to be felt so we can know when it's time to let go of what's harming us so we can begin again, so we can keep growing. Maybe the shell-ish version of us isn't really us at all. Maybe it's what we need to leave behind so we can move forward.

I've been thinking about this a lot. The points where I've felt so empty as a mom have been when I've felt squeezed so hard I could barely breathe, with no hope it would end anytime soon. Mothering has, at certain points, been all-out exhausting, and at times it's been utterly hopeless. These periods have marked my memory much like the births and adoptions of our children. The arrival of each one of our children was marked as a monumentally happy moment, while these difficult seasons of motherhood were equally monumental in a not-so-happy way.

In those times, I pulled back and set the pace of my life to a slower rhythm only out of sheer necessity. My body wasn't physically able to keep up. My heart wasn't either. I felt like I would die if I didn't slow down. I stopped serving in leadership, attending Bible study, writing, being with friends, and reaching out. It wasn't a giving up; I was filling back up.

It was a filling by emptying. If you've ever been completely overwhelmed by life, you most likely know your rescue and recovery certainly won't come by busyness or overserving, that's for sure.

What if instead of waiting until I was lifeless on the floor, I'd taken notice of the warning signs and learned to rescue my own life for once? What if I had called in some reinforcements, lightened my load, or asked for help before I could hardly breathe?

Just as it doesn't for the snake, the big squeeze for us doesn't just appear. It's gradual, intensifying a little bit more each day. Our lives don't appear too full overnight. Except for in extreme cases, our proverbial plates aren't heaped to overflowing because of a single decision or circumstance. We make one choice after another, add one more responsibility or one more activity, and perhaps perform one more rescue we aren't meant to take on.

The hustling.

The driving.

The planning.

The caring.

The responsibility.

The multitasking.

The worry.

The wait.

The stress.

The thinking.

The needs.

The lack.

The helping.

The weariness.

The fear.

The snapping.

Before we can even figure out how we got to this place, we already know something must change. Can life be breathed into such a lifeless form?

Do you want the bad news first? There isn't exactly a permanent fix. But the good news is we can alleviate some of the burden we seem to always be carrying and bring our shell-like forms back to life.

Sometimes that means taking a long hard look at our life and the way we're living it.

Is it possible to be distracted by meeting needs? Yes.

Is it possible to be distracted by serving in that role no one else will fill? Yes.

Is it possible to be distracted by how helping others makes us feel and appear? Yes.

Is it possible our overserving in certain areas is robbing another person of their God-given role? Yes.

Is it possible we fear a bare-bones schedule? Yes.

Is it possible to fill up with too many good things? Yes.

Is it possible to simultaneously take care of everyone and everything *and* your own needs? *No.* No, it isn't.

It isn't generous or valiant to run ourselves into the ground in the name of serving others or in the name of working hard or staying busy. On paper it sounds crazy to serve or work to the point of not functioning, but how often do we do this? *Way too often.*

It isn't selfless of us to take care of everyone else if our own mental and physical health are falling to pieces. It's dangerous.

When should we give and when should we spend time gearing back up? Where's the line? When is the proper time to give, to rest, and then refuel?

These are questions we must answer, because we can't keep putting ourselves in last place. We need to be the ones rescued for once.

6

The Givers and Their Guilt

Amanda

Each one must give as he has decided in his heart,
not reluctantly or under compulsion, for God loves a cheerful giver.

2 CORINTHIANS 9:7

Moms are classic givers.

We give ourselves the last plate of food, the last piece of cake (not counting the one we snuck in the corner of the kitchen earlier), and we're usually the last one in bed at night. We're the take-care-ers and the queens of *Don't-worry-I'll-get-it*. We're always putting our needs dead last.

We're perpetually putting off a haircut, a friend date, one of those lovely annual doctor's appointments, and a few new pairs of good underwear. Things that bring us sanity and well-being are constantly put on the back burner. We'll get to them eventually, we say. But what if we made it a point to do those things?

May: new underwear

June: coffee with Mary

July: the dentist

August: haircut

Not exactly exciting, but necessary.

Taking care of ourselves doesn't just mean we should take care of the outer body, which the Bible says is wasting away or perishing. It also means we're the caretakers of our souls, the inner, non-perishing, and immortal part of our being. Second Corinthians 4:16 says that because of our faith, we should not lose heart, because "though our outer self is wasting away, our inner self is being renewed day by day."

Our inner self, our soul—the part that can't decay—is being renewed and strengthened daily by God. Is it possible to block that renewal by our own power? It seems like we could be our own barrier to soul refreshment by packing in too much—more than was ever meant to fill our days. As Emily P. Freeman says, "The soul and the schedule don't follow the same rules."[1]

We love helping others, but our bodies and souls must drop the guilt when we need to take care of ourselves. Taking care of ourselves is good. Necessary. Reviving. But our busy lives sap the energies God gives us to go about *His* business.

On the first day of a new Bible study, we participants each shared a bit about ourselves. It was a mixed group of women of all ages, from the young mom to the aging empty nester. We told about our families and how we spent our days. Two of the women's answers stuck with me long after leaving the church. When sharing what they enjoyed doing, both of their voices lowered as they "confessed" they loved to read. One shared how earlier in the week she had laid on the couch in the middle of the day (gasp) with a blanket and a book. She couldn't remember the last time she had done that.

The other said reading was her "guilty pleasure." Reading? *Guilty?* I don't know what sort of books she's reading, but I can almost guarantee her guilt is less about what genre she chooses than about spending time engaged in something she doesn't consider productive, like taking care of someone else.

Guilt seemed to be hanging heavy over both women simply because they didn't always use their time to do something for someone else. *I should be skipping out on me, not on them,* we think. So we get up off the couch and fold the blanket, place the proverbial book back on the shelf, and release the prolonged sigh of someone longing for rest. We need rest, but should we take it when we can be taking care of others?

That's where the conflict begins for us. *How do I take care of me and them?*

God's Word speaks to all this through the life of Jesus. In John 13 we see Jesus serving as He washes His disciples' feet. But then in Luke 5:16 we see Jesus withdraw from others to pray, which speaks to us about picking our worn-out life off the floor in the form of prayer and retreat. And in John 15:1-17 we learn from Jesus about the imperative of abiding in the Father.

We might say to ourselves, *I can't be like Jesus. Jesus was never a mother. He doesn't know what it's like to have people pulling at His clothes, whining, wanting to be fed, and following Him everywhere. I can't just leave and go pray whenever I want.*

Oh wait. Jesus basically "mothered" a band of misfits everywhere He went during His ministry. He totally knew what mothering felt like; He took care of His disciples and the people who always seemed to be lingering around Him. But He let Himself rest too. Rest was a high priority. Communion with His Father took the top spot.

Here's my paraphrase of how Jesus might have sounded in our culture today: "Guys, I'm going over there to be by Myself now. I'll meet you later."

That's like one of my classic lines to my kids: "Guys, I'm stepping out to the front yard to take this phone call. Please don't follow me." Or "I'm heading up to use the restroom. Please don't come knocking."

To take care of Himself and His soul, Jesus set boundaries for the people in His life, and He set dates for just Him and His Father. He gave; He retreated. He spoke; He prayed. He served; He refueled. He did all this with pure and clear thinking, never under negative compulsion. Jesus walked in love, not guilt.

Are we following His pattern? Or are we giving out of guilt?

Jesus never served because He *had* to. He gave of His life because He *wanted* to. Many, many times I've been guilted into giving my time. But as I've grown and processed my decision-making habits through the years, I've learned to think ahead and imagine my life in a week, a month, or even a year, and then ask myself, *Is guilt enough to sustain me and help carry out the commitment I've made?* The answer is usually no, because guilt lacks passion and is therefore unable to maintain an extended period of guilt-driven service.

Think of the Sunday school teacher who volunteered to teach each week for an entire year because no one else seemed interested and she'd already said no to helping at vacation Bible school and running a women's Bible study. You can almost guarantee she's going to be doing a lot of soul-searching by mid-January. Guilt can drive us to do a lot of things, but saying yes because we feel obligated rather than invigorated by an opportunity can hurt more than it helps.

Wise decision making and a gentle no can take us further than guilt ever could. Sometimes we need to say no to good things so we can say yes to better things.

1

It's All Good

Anne-Renee

How we spend our days is, of course, how we spend our lives.
Annie Dillard[1]

Last week I was looking at my calendar for the month and noticed every square had been filled:

A field trip
A snack I'd promised to bring
Hosting a midweek dinner for our small group at church
Worship practice
Coffee with a friend
A meal for a new mom

Plus all the regular activities, such as work, Bible study, youth group, dentist appointments, haircuts, and birthdays. All good things. Beneficial things. Things I knew would buoy the hearts of those involved. But oh my word, how did that many activities creep into our family's schedule?

Busyness seems to be the defining soundtrack to many of our lives. It's not that what we're doing in and of itself is wrong, but maybe the timing is off.

As an old music professor of mine was wont to say, "Timing is everything." Poorly timed pursuits can be damaging to our families and relationships, not to mention to our souls.

When my son was only two months old and my daughter was nearing her second birthday, I agreed to be part of the leadership team for our local MOPS group. (Those initials stand for Mothers Of Preschoolers, not what I first assumed they stood for: a cleaning society.)

I dreamed, and planned, and typed copious notes for our group of gals. Naptime and evenings found me making little gifts for our table leaders and attempting to manufacture more ways to reach the hearts of our moms.

I must admit, I was slightly obsessed about making everything perfect, using all my energies to encourage others. Meanwhile, my own little family suffered from my sudden emotional and mental disappearing act. *Now you see me, now you don't.* My sweet little toddler daughter launched a regular whining routine for me to read to her or play a game, begging and whimpering for my attention, while piles of laundry multiplied in my absence.

Now, the fresh new leadership position was good for me, the fellowship was sweet, and the adult conversation was much needed. But the timing was off. I became the mom who was consistently too busy. Too busy to listen to silly dreams over the breakfast table. Too busy to play dress up. Too busy to cuddle a little missy with her favorite book after naptime. And much too busy for a pint-sized sous chef to help in the hurried task of making meals. I became so preoccupied with my new role that I forgot about my existing one: Mom.

I became so preoccupied with my new role that I forgot about my existing one: Mom.

I was giving away efforts that should have been employed elsewhere; more specifically, at home. But in my eagerness and enthusiasm for the new, I was too blind to see it. I was desperate for fellowship and appreciation, hungry for something outside our seemingly claustrophobic four walls. Those are healthy desires, but I was practicing unhealthy habits in pursuit of them.

I'll never forget the day my sleepy daughter sauntered into the upstairs room I was in after her nap, her blankie and stuffed puppy in tow, asking for cereal. I snapped at her, telling her Mama was too busy to help her right then, and she was old enough to get her own snack. She didn't need *me* to do everything for her!

Minutes passed without further inquiry or interruption. And then I heard a huge crash.

I panicked, calling my daughter's name while racing down the steps (which now seemed like the longest staircase known to man). I found her safe and sound, sitting on the floor of the kitchen pantry, surrounded by mini mountains of spilled cereal. Big gulps and tears accompanied her little voice-cracked apologies, her tiny heart crushed with the weight of her mama's mean words.

The reality of my own selfishness was now glaringly evident in those unwelcome piles of cereal beckoning me to clean them up. It was a glorious mess of my own making. It wasn't my daughter's fault; it was mine and mine alone.

Honestly, just writing this story brings back all that same heavy mom guilt and shame. If only I'd chosen a better moment to be distracted by what seemed to be such a good thing!

I sincerely wish with all my heart that I could hit Rewind on the regrets that multiply in moments like these. And yet beyond the guilty conscience and penitence, I can learn from these moments, from the precious gift I should have been taking better care of—that sleepy-eyed little girl with a rumbly tummy, sitting defeated in a puddle of Cheerios.

What a dilemma—so many good things and simply not enough time to do them. It's a categorizing of sorts, a contest to see what and who will win over our affections and our calendars. What we're doing can appear productive and generous at heart, but is *now* the proper time for it?

Is right now the right time?

That's a hard question to ask ourselves. It makes us squirm, looking up at the ceiling to avoid the uncomfortable feeling it evokes deep inside. (I say this with all the kindness and remorse of a mama who has made the wrong choice time and time again.)

I have flooded my mind with *all* the excuses, trying to justify doing and pursuing things outside my post and outside God's timetable for our family. I still struggle with this, for I am a woman who likes to be appreciated. I *love* for others to articulate their affirmation and to assign value to what I'm doing. But children don't often express appreciation. They don't usually thank you for taking care of them, driving them to-and-fro, making their meals, doing their laundry, wiping their noses and bottoms, or even giving them life, for goodness' sake. But I'm slowly learning to sift through my tendency to make excuses.

If we want to be intentional with the people and tasks God has put before us, we must learn to weigh the right time with the wrong time and right things with the wrong things. Because God desires the best for His children—for our good, and His glory.

8

What Kind of Yes Is It, Anyway?

Anne-Renee

Don't just say yes because you're tired of saying no.

JJ HELLER[1]

I used to think I had to say yes to everything. If someone asked me to do something, then clearly, the Lord God above wanted me to do it. I didn't question it. I didn't complain about it. I simply assumed that what was being asked of me was my right-now assignment.

But occasionally, my yes would give birth to a whole litter of squirmy misgivings. No sooner would I say, *Yup, I can do that,* than a crazy little phenomenon would begin to take place: Overwhelming stress. Fatigue or illness. Forgetfulness. Anxiousness. Or the sickening feeling deep in the pit of my stomach that I really should have said no.

Worse, I'd be afraid I'd lose out on a wonderful opportunity because I had already committed myself. Oh, the horror! Especially if the new opportunity was something I really wanted to do.

Then I'd start second-guessing myself. *Maybe I shouldn't have agreed to do this. Does God feel disappointed in my choice? Should I back out now? Maybe someone else is better suited. I bet they're wishing they'd never asked me! Will I miss out on something else God specially equipped me for?*

It seems like we're always and forever selling someone short—either ourselves or someone else. And as we've been learning, every choice has a cost, a trade-off of sorts.

As a convalescing people pleaser, I want everyone to be happy—with the process, with the outcome, but especially with me and my role in whatever is going on. Yet we can't please everyone, and God doesn't tell us in His Word to do *all* things. He tells us to rejoice always, to pray always, and to give thanks always (1 Thessalonians 5:16-18).

Nowhere in Scripture do I find a command to say yes to everyone who asks us to do something, nor any verses that say we should do all things at all times for all people under the sun. God is a good Father and desires good things for His children. He knows we would burn out in a state of physical, mental, and emotional exhaustion if we agreed to do absolutely everything everyone asked of us. He didn't create us to do it all, build it all, or achieve it all. To greet everyone on Sunday morning as they walk into church, teach a class, help with worship (both in the big service and in children's church), preach the sermon, give the altar call, *and* serve the coffee.

If you can do all those things every Sunday, week in and week out, you have my admiration and full attention. Congratulations, you are the most amazing human being I've ever come across! But the body of Christ wasn't meant to be like Bert from *Mary Poppins*, combining an entire orchestra into a one-man band.

We have different talents, callings, and purposes, and we're hand-crafted to reflect the uniqueness and creativity of our master creator. Romans 12:6-8 says,

> Having gifts that differ according to the grace given to us, let us use them: if prophecy, in proportion to our faith; if service, in our serving; the one who teaches, in his teaching; the one who exhorts, in his exhortation; the one who contributes, in generosity; the one who leads, with zeal; the one who does acts of mercy, with cheerfulness.

How in the world do we know what we should agree to and what we should say no to?

How do we avoid letting the demands of others dictate our answers, pulling us away from what God has specifically designed for us?

It may sound trite to some, but I suggest we begin with prayer. Then after we've laid the issue before the Lord, let's bathe it thoroughly in Scripture. Think of bathing a baby. You have to address every little crook and chubby wrinkle.

Let's ask ourselves,

Who will be blessed?

Who will get the glory?

Am I passionate about this?

What is my motive for saying yes?

Is this even feasible? Realistically? Physically? Emotionally? Spiritually?

And if we're still unsure,

Who might be a wise source of counsel to chat with about this?

Maybe now is not the right season. Or this should be a short-term rather than a long-term agreement. Do our current yeses and noes reflect where we think God is leading us in the long term?

All these little yeses can add up quickly. As we only have one life here on this earth, we want to be wise stewards of the time God has allotted us. As children of the light, we want to be intentional with our schedules and deliberate in our choices.

Now, what happens if we think we should pass on an opportunity? How do we graciously say no? My non-confrontational heart cringes at the thought of telling someone I can't help them.

That's where I must come back to the gifts Paul mentions in Romans 12:6-8. We're all different, and rightly so. I'm not helping anyone if I can't give them 100 percent of my efforts and energies.

Not only that, but what if I'm robbing someone else of the joy of doing this assignment? Maybe God has called someone else to say yes to this request. I don't want to get in the way of God at work! Like you,

I want to be purposeful about the people and tasks God puts before me, giving them my all and absolute best.

I love how Lysa TerKeurst puts it in her book *The Best Yes*: "Saying yes all the time won't make me Wonder Woman. It will make me a worn-out woman."[2] And as many a burned-out mom can attest, too much of a good thing is still too much.

Too much of a good thing is still too much.

All the Good Things

Right Things, Wrong Times

To Remember

- We need to be the ones rescued for once.
- Sometimes we have to say no to good things, so we can say yes to better things.
- We don't want to become so preoccupied with new roles that we forget about our existing ones.
- Let's ask ourselves, *Is right now the right time?*

To Hold On To

Rejoice always, pray without ceasing, give thanks in all circumstances; for this is the will of God in Christ Jesus for you (1 Thessalonians 5:16-18).

Though our outer self is wasting away, our inner self is being renewed day by day (2 Corinthians 4:16).

To Consider

- How would you formulate your own rescue plan?
- What's one way you could breathe well this week?

Part Three

The Important and Everything Else

9

What I Want Most

Amanda

Discipline is choosing between what you want
now and what you want most.

ANONYMOUS

I sat on the edge of my unmade bed, searching Pinterest for ideas for our home remodel with half of my brain. The other half tried to decipher if the shouts and banging coming from the living room were worth getting up to check. Was that happy or argumentative shouting? Playful or destructive banging? It was hard to tell. Did I really want to know? If it was a relatively harmless argument, shouldn't I let the kids work it out themselves?

The pull was strong to keep my Pinterest search alive, and the urge to investigate what might be going on out there in no-man's land was virtually nonexistent. There was bound to be something I needed to address—a behavior that needed modifying—but I just didn't think I had it in me. The apps on my phone seemed like a much happier place to spend these minutes. I could scroll and tap my way to a flawless imaginary home, or I could go out there and grow my very own tension headache. *Hmm...tough choice.*

It actually *was* a tough choice, because parenting was calling. Was I going to let it go to voice mail even though I'm perfectly capable (and responsible) to answer the call? Why was this so hard? What had happened to me?

When did my desire to attentively involve myself and help my kids fall into second place behind my desire to do what I want, when I want? I don't know when the switch happened, but once I realized it, I despised it and everything about it. My phone and other tools-turned-interruptions had become enemies, not the friends I thought they'd been.

Have you ever considered throwing your phone, computer, or other device across the room one second, and then wanted to coddle it and touch it and engage with it so much that you wouldn't dare let it go the next?

I must scroll through Instagram just one more time. Yes, I must. What exactly am I looking for anyway?

Something interesting might be on Facebook at this very moment. One of my friends I haven't seen in 20 years might be posting something. Huh? I mean, that's not what I'm saying to myself when I get on there, but what else am I expecting to find?

The draw to temporarily escape the realities of life seems to plague me most when I need to do something important, like sleep, make dinner, work, look my kids in the eye, or say, write this book. Interacting with the apps on my phone at the wrong times and for the wrong reasons serves as only a temporary high, leaving me frustrated with myself.

It's sort of like a sugar high. Consuming a sugary something feels satisfying in the moment, but it has few lasting benefits, if any. Unless you call gaining ten pounds in one summer from consuming too many treats beneficial. *Ahem.* Or a daily spike and then drop in blood sugar leaving you feeling tired and sad. That's fun too.

Why do we so often go back to the temporarily satisfying places if they make us feel so bad?

Why do we so often go back to the temporarily satisfying places if they make us feel so bad?

The science behind it has to do with the dopamine reward system, which is sometimes called the compulsion loop. Science teaches us that a person's brain doesn't fully mature until age 25 *(whoa)*, so that explains a few things about the teen years and those after high school when we might not have used the best judgment. I was married and had my first two children within that zone, and I gape in amazement at that. My brain wasn't fully mature? How come no one told us? How many of us were or are walking around mothering without a mature brain? It's funny, yet staggering at the same time.

All this talk about loops and rewards has me thinking about us moms. We so often get caught in the same cycles with the same negative effects, fully mature brains or not.

At this very moment, my hand is twitching to reach for my phone. My mind keeps going there, and I have to refocus every few minutes. I posted something on Instagram 30 minutes ago, and my mind can't forget about it. My hand wants to grab my phone to find out who saw it or responded. Why? Why can't I relax like a normal person and just check it when I'm done writing? And why is it so important for me to know what my post is up to without me?

Writing for this book when I have the time set aside is the best choice for me. If I check my phone 12 hours from now, what I'm looking for now will still be there. But if I wait 12 hours to write, my window of writing time will be gone.

Raise your hand if you know *exactly* what I'm talking about. I know many of us struggle to stay focused. I also know many of us have a hard time sticking with the good and worthy pursuits right in front of us:

Building our relationship with God.

Studying the Bible alone or in a group.

Investing in our most important people.

Looking those same people in the eye and really listening and conversing.

Giving mindful attention to our work, from home or elsewhere.

Keeping our home clean and functioning.

Making meals.

Having friends.

Helping others.

If we know these things and more are of utmost importance, how can we help ourselves keep them in their proper place? What is it with our craving right-now pleasure that offers no lasting promises?

A lot of this cycle has to do with our brains and the reward hit of dopamine, as I mentioned before. We experience and enjoy a nice and addicting sensation each time we receive a like, comment, or any other happy response from our time online. It keeps us coming back for more. Brains and chemicals aside, it's a spiritual issue too. The Enemy loves keeping us distracted, and as I mentioned in chapter 1, this shiny, inviting world we live in isn't an excuse for allowing ourselves to stay distracted, but it can make it that much easier.

Ephesians 5:15-17 says, "Look carefully then how you walk, not as unwise but as wise, making the best use of the time, because the days are evil. Therefore do not be foolish, but understand what the will of the Lord is." This scripture sounds as though the apostle Paul was talking about our times. But ways for humans to stay distracted have always been with us, and so has the enemy of our souls.

Proverbs 5:8 says, "Keep your way far from her, and do not go near the door of her house." This proverb is speaking about avoiding an adulteress and the places she dwells if you're tempted, but I believe it applies here as well. Anything that tempts us to fall into sinful patterns should be avoided. In our case, distraction could be the "her" in this verse.

What might it look like for us to heed this warning in Proverbs?

Let's use phones and the internet as our example. Avoiding temptation might look like:

- charging our device in a room other than the one where
  we're spending time with our family

- setting our device on a shelf when we don't need it

- planning a time for that web search we've been meaning
  to do and set a timer to keep ourselves from getting lost
  on a trail of web pages

- looking up and setting the distraction aside when someone speaks to us

- removing addictive apps from our phones and tablets, or
  saving them for times when they won't distract us from
  our real lives

- choosing a set number of times for checking notifications
  and apps each day and sticking to it (for example, 9:00
  a.m., 1:00 p.m., and 6:00 p.m., 15 minutes each time)

- setting timers for internet-related tasks to help bring us
  back to reality

- designating one or more days a week to use our phones
  strictly for calling and texting

- taking a weekly day off from all apps and websites

If our main distraction is something other than phones and the
internet, we can brainstorm ways to avoid that temptation as well.
What will help us be less likely to engage in what makes us feel miserable when all is said and done?

What do we want most? What is keeping us from that? Discipline is a learned skill, one we must practice to improve. It's imperative we find a way around what hijacks our minds, because what we
want most is waiting.

10

A Long Stay in Temporary Land

Amanda

The LORD our God spoke to us at Horeb,
saying, "You have stayed long enough at this mountain."

DEUTERONOMY 1:6 NRSV

W e recently moved into a fixer-upper straight out of 1987. Dark wood, popcorn ceilings, brown linoleum—you name it. But it was priced right and on a gorgeous piece of property with a creek, gardens, tons of trees, and space to roam. When our offer was chosen out of the handful the sellers were presented, we were frozen with the possibility of buyer's remorse. The house, with only two bedrooms and one bathroom, needed a complete overhaul to accommodate the ten of us. It was perfect for the retired couple who lived there alone, but it was not as ideal for our crew of four boys, four girls, and two parents.

Yet we had vision. The empty concrete and cinder-block basement and the two-car garage could both be remodeled to hold more bedrooms, a family room, laundry facilities, and a great big bathroom. The place had so much potential—and we had so much work to do.

The upstairs "finished" portion—after the removal of a couple of walls, that is—would get a complete cosmetic overhaul as well. New paint, scraped popcorn ceilings, and new flooring. A completely new kitchen here and a shiplap wall (or three) there.

We worked ourselves bone-weary all summer. Between both of us working and taking care of kids on break from school, our hours for remodeling were few. Whenever we got the chance, we hauled everyone over to the new house 30 minutes away, stopping at the store first so we'd have something there to eat. It was a nonstop routine of driving, working, and making meals in the middle of the dust, mess, and kids.

Other than a few trips to our neighborhood pool back at our rental, no summer fun was to be had. We worked and worked the months away. I think we took one day off and did something fun, but I can't remember what it was.

Right in the middle of all this, we experienced two back-to-back car accidents within three weeks of each other. One of them totaled the vehicle we had just paid off. Tensions were high, to say the least.

The month of August came. To halt paying both rent and a mortgage and driving two hours a day back and forth to school (the younger children had to change schools again, just one year after our initial move to North Carolina), we chose to end the lease on our rental. We spent weeks packing and slowly moving belongings to the shed at the new house, as well as getting the rental back to the sparkly state we found it in. At the end of all that and a summer of remodeling, we were completely spent. Completely done.

But we couldn't be done. This was just the beginning.

The ten of us sucked in a bunch of air, plugged our noses, and then leapt into the murky waters of living in the middle of a remodel with only one bathroom, stick-frame walls, and construction dust everywhere. It was time to live in our extremely unfinished home at the end of the cul-de-sac across town.

The kids slept on their mattresses on the floor, the four boys in the garage-turned-future-dining-room and the four girls in the one bedroom that had any semblance of being finished. That bedroom still had the purple walls and brown carpet it came with. Each kid had their own cardboard box to hold some clothes, along with a favorite possession and a book or two. The master bedroom's walls were stripped down to the studs, and pink insulation hung out of the ceiling. And we had one lonely lightbulb that hung from a few wires to light our way. We knew it wouldn't be our living situation forever, but it sure wasn't easy.

Because we cut our expenses, we could use that money to keep working on the house, doing the bulk of the work ourselves. We could make it better. It would be extremely slow going—but at least it would be going.

Sometimes I sat on the edge of my bed with the splintery and dusty subfloor staring back at me and wondered how in the world we got here. But even in this mess, I couldn't get past the fact that we were living at a higher standard than most of the world's population. How could I be sad about that? Our kids were seeing life in a whole new light. The conveniences they'd been accustomed to were no longer available. I loved this for them.

Yet even though our home wasn't pretty, we had clean and filtered water. A working stovetop and oven. A dishwasher. A washer and dryer in the downstairs construction zone after just one month without either of those appliances. A brand-new heating and cooling system. Food. Togetherness. And we were free. Free to buy and build and make a home for ourselves without persecution of any kind.

Yeah, we had holes in walls and missing walls, and eventually we were gifted leftover red church carpet remnants to temporarily cover that horrible subfloor. The projects were endless, and we couldn't seem to find enough time to work on them.

In all that time living like that, though, I couldn't bring myself to shed a tear over it. What was a temporary, yearlong situation for us would be a dream come true for billions of others. What was a hardship for us would be the big break and life-changing rescue so many are desperate for.

Truly, how could I be sad about that?

Our high standards of living mean nothing when so many people in the world literally *have nothing*, and their children are dying because of it.

It's not always our circumstances that bring us down; sometimes just our thoughts about them crumple us. We think we'll "die" without our preferred comforts. But the truth is our high standards and general snobbiness are killing us—just not in the way we think.

How will our chosen priorities shape our kids? How will our attitudes toward the temporary trappings taught in the Bible shape us? By watching and listening to us, what will they learn is most important in life?

Second Corinthians 4:17-18 says, "This light momentary affliction is preparing for us an eternal weight of glory beyond all comparison, as we look not to the things that are seen but to the things that are unseen. For the things that are seen are transient, but the things that are unseen are eternal."

Even when Scripture tells us to leave everything to follow Jesus (He tells us that in His own words), we don't. We cling to our goods, neighborhoods, and status in the community and say, *Nuh-uh. I'll go to church and love people, but I'm not giving anything up for You, God. I'm not going to live like You say I should. You don't understand what I need.*

Plenty of distractions haunt us day in and day out. We can set those aside when we're truly disciplined about it, but what about the bigger things we can't set aside so easily? We can tuck our phones into our purses or up on a shelf, but what about the fleeting pleasure of wealth, status, and materialism?

What about our obsession with retirement funds and college savings for our kids? Does that hit you in a tender spot? I realize this is a book about learning to live undistracted in mothering, but our over-all mind-set affects everything. But too often our goals become our gods, and their distraction becomes our way of life.

Our goals become our gods.

These things can hold our attention in unhealthy ways when we think our circumstances, houses, closets, or bank accounts must be at a certain level for us to be happy. My account must have X number of dollars, and my closet needs the newest clothes, and everyone needs to think I'm something special in my beautiful home.

Why? I mean *really*, why? Some of us get so used to operating at a certain level and with a certain budget that it's hard to imagine life any other way.

Living in the middle of a full and drastic remodel job has taught me so much. Whether I'm living in a construction zone or a fully ren-ovated home, my priorities shouldn't change. God and my family are still my top priorities. My problems won't go away magically when the flooring's in and the walls are patched and painted.

When our house remodel is finished, I'll still be me, and my fam-ily will be the same. But my perspective will have the opportunity for change when the comforts of life aren't the goal anymore. We were never meant to stay too long in temporary lands. The Israelites expe-rienced this while they were wandering from place to place in search of the next great thing, the promised land, and we're no different.

Too many things that won't last seem to suck us in and steal our time, offering nothing in return but loads of disappointment. Eter-nal things draw us closer while temporary things can draw us away.

Eternal things draw us closer while temporary things can draw us away.

I love the way John speaks plainly in 1 John 2:15-17:

Do not love the world or the things in the world. If anyone loves the world, the love of the Father is not in him.
For all that is in the world—the desires of the flesh and
the desires of the eyes and pride of life—is not from the
Father but is from the world. And the world is passing
away along with its desires, but whoever does the will of
God abides forever.

The world is passing away with all its desires, so if everything is
passing away except the human soul, that should be a directional sign
for us. We should spend our time there.

II

That Elusive Fine Line

Anne-Renee

*The first step in crafting the life you want is
to get rid of everything you don't.*

JOSHUA BECKER[1]

Ever since I was a young girl, I've often thought of life as a rickety balancing scale, performing a delicate sifting, weighing what matters against what doesn't. The kind of scale with two pans suspended with chains on either end of a beam, each one going up or down at the slightest change of weight in one or the other.

Now, if this girlish notion were true and life was indeed a scale, where would what we do and pursue every day sit? Would the two pans sit evenly between the unimportant and valuable?

It's such a hard balance, this estimation of the eternal and the temporary, a calculation of priceless and precious in contrast with the worthless and unimportant. Who's to say which is which? Who is to define what is important and what is unimportant in our lives?

While I was growing up, my parents put a great deal of importance on the tradition of having dinner together as a family—each night, every day, all week long. Of course, the occasional basketball game or music concert interrupted our evening routine, but for the most part, six o'clock found my whole family gathered around my parents' brown, faux-wood Formica table, sometimes with an extra friend or two, but always, always together. Heads bowed. Hands connected. Paused hearts giving thanks.

I'm sure my siblings and I fought against the mandatory togetherness from time to time. I'm doubly sure we rolled our eyes at the required time out of our own selfish mind-sets to focus on one another. But in hindsight, I recognize the wisdom of those moments—the hilarity, the richness, the incredible value.

We want our scales to tip toward the important. The life-giving. The thought-provoking. The day-to-day things that change our hearts and bring hope to those around us. This is where it begins—assessing what fills our lives and infiltrates our planners, those occurrences that bring value and worth to our every day. The time spent in the Word, prayerful conversations with God, sweet fellowship with friends, and those meaningful moments around the table with our families.

If I were to ask you what mattered, what truly mattered for you, what would you say? My guess is you wouldn't mention growing your retirement account, buying your own private island, or moving to a bigger house in a nicer neighborhood.

In his book *Spiritual Rhythm,* Mark Buchanan writes about the importance of making these kinds of determinations each day:

> The examen is a form of personal inventory. At day's end, spend time in prayerful reflection on your day: your comings and goings, routines and disruptions, work and play, discoveries and disappointments. Think about who you met, or missed. Think about your moments of aloneness. In all, ask two questions: when was I most alive, most present, most filled and fulfilled today? And when was I most taxed, stressed, distracted, depleted today? A simpler, and more spiritually focused, version of those questions: when did I feel closest to God, and when farthest?[2]

Sometimes people quiz themselves to help them sift through things in life, weighing substance against significance. They ask heart-revealing questions like…

If I had only one week (or one month or year) to live, how would I use my last days here on earth?

What would I tell my family and friends?

What would I change? Confess? Forgive? Let go?

To whom would I say, "I love you"?

With whom would I share the good news of Christ's sacrifice and forgiveness?

What would I add to my bucket list? Travel? Service? Skydiving?

These types of questions make us want to find those moments that matter and then make those moments a reality.

Find those moments that matter and then make those moments a reality.

Jesus once helped a rich young ruler do a life evaluation of this sort, helping him to see what mattered and what didn't. And in true Son of God form, He didn't just hand out the answers; He spoke in questions and imparted truth with challenges.

The secret sifting tool He shared with the man was this: "Go, sell all that you have and give to the poor, and you will have treasure in heaven; and come, follow me" (Mark 10:21).

He gave him five simple acts:

Go.

Sell.

Give.

Come.

Follow.

Five acts that on their own don't sound all that earth-shattering, but Jesus understood what hardships the youthful ruler was facing.

He knew the hold material possessions can have on a person, how difficult it is to stay focused on God when monetary pressures and responsibilities urge us elsewhere.

Jesus's life-changing directive was given to the young man by putting it into an eternal equation with a mathematical answer the man couldn't quite swallow. Oh, if only all that wealth hadn't been in his way! Mark 10:22 says he was "disheartened by the saying" and "went away sorrowful, for he had great possessions."

My heart aches for this young man. He was rubbing elbows with such greatness and holiness but was unable to taste the sweetness of oneness with God. Seeing all those dusty, uneducated disciples hanging around Jesus, but somehow left outside the cool kids' circle because of his unwillingness to give up wealth, position, power, and prestige.

We begin to see that this delicate balance isn't just about things, but about living lives pleasing to the Father. Lives that long to bring Him glory. Lives that yearn to be one with Him and with His purpose for us here on earth.

And so, we sift. We weigh. We measure. We balance. We release and let go. And we count our daily to-dos and calculate our actions by asking ourselves if they matter. Do they matter to those around us? And most importantly, do they matter to God?

In so doing, we choose to fill our lives with significance. With value. Saying no to obstacles and whatever distracts us, no to anything that could get in the way of our relationship with the Father and our desire to live out the Great Commission. We begin to hold time and comfort and money and status with a loose, open hand.

We choose the hard but the good. The unselfish. The sacrificial. The soul filling. The priceless. The kind of life where our pockets may be empty, but our hearts are overflowing, filled with the knowledge of an extraordinary peace and a sacrificial love.

Filled with the stuff that truly matters.

12

We're All Seeking Something

Anne-Renee

*Change is a part of each person's story as assuredly
as the sun is a part of each new sunrise.*

KRISTEN STRONG[1]

I remember the first time I heard it—*really* heard it: The call to do something beyond myself, to seek someone else's good and not my own.

I was a self-absorbed, self-serving college student, working my way through the university educational system, working hard yet learning only for myself. Don't worry. I also carved out plenty of time for fun, making sure my daily routine included a late-night Rollerblade session with my bestest buddy and roommate, Jane.

The previous summer I'd been waitressing at a guest ranch in Montana, a gorgeous setting with great benefits and phenomenal pay. By Christmas, I was already dreaming of returning to that breathtaking scenery and magnificent mountains. Think *A River Runs Through It* meets *The Horse Whisperer*, a majestic stage filled with rugged, jaw-dropping beauty everywhere you looked.

Then something happened over Christmas break. At the last minute I agreed to attend a Campus Crusade conference with one of my brothers. As I sat in my comfy hotel ballroom chair, sipping lemon water and listening to speakers and participating in some amazing heartfelt worship, I heard God speak:

This is what I have for you.

That was it. One phrase. I had no idea what it meant or what I should do with it. It just hung there, playing on Repeat in my mind. I wrote it down in my session notes and then tried to forget about it. It just seemed too big. Too scary. Too unknown and ambiguous. And definitely too far out of my comfort zone.

But I didn't want to be a disobedient daughter, so I started lackadaisically praying, asking God what in the world He wanted me to do. Of course, in characteristic God fashion, He made it so plain that I couldn't say no, couldn't wiggle out of it, and couldn't come up with any excuse why I shouldn't follow exactly where He was directing me to go. Another speaker went to the front of the room and started talking on the topic, "Where Is God Calling You?" As he was giving information about where Campus Crusade was equipping saints and sharing the gospel, he was flashing PowerPoint photos of different locations throughout the world. When he put up a picture of New York City, I heard it again:

This is what I have for you.

As you can imagine, the naïve, suburban middle-class girl that I was started arguing with the Lord of the universe immediately. *Are You kidding me, God? Do You know how dangerous the streets of New York are? I mean, there's no way my parents are going to let me go on a trip like this. The crime rates alone will have them shutting down this request at the first mention of where I'd be staying. I mean, talk about Ghetto-ville. Plus, I'd be making absolutely no money for college…and this whole Summer in the City idea costs money. A lot of money. Money, that as You well know, I do not have. So I'm sorry, Lord, but this is not even a feasible choice for me. This can't be what You meant in saying, "This is what I have for you." Surely You were talking about something else. Or maybe*

*You were talking to someone else and I just happened to overhear. Yup,
that must be it.*

Problem solved. Case closed.

I had become so distracted by everything I was trying to accomplish and all the plans I had for *my* life, that I couldn't see why God
would want to throw a whole monkey wrench into the perfect blue-
prints I'd already laid out for myself.

Proverbs 16:9 describes this truth so perfectly: "The heart of man
plans his way, but the LORD establishes his steps."

Let me tell you…I had planned. I had prepared. I had it all laid
out. But here was God trying to direct me elsewhere. Urging me
down another path where I needed to seek Him and His righteousness, not seek me and my own selfishness.

**The more I dug into God's Word, the more I realized how
out of alignment my plans and priorities were.**

The more I dug into God's Word, the more I realized how out of
alignment my plans and priorities were. Like, way off. Matthew 6:33
says, "Seek first the kingdom of God and *his* righteousness" (emphasis mine). His kingdom? What about me and my life plans?

The rest of that verse says, "And all these things will be added to
you." What things? Money for college? A home with a white picket
fence, one husband, one dog, and 2.4 kids?

Just a few verses earlier, in verse 24 Jesus says, "No one can serve
two masters." Ouch. Now we were getting personal. Really personal.

Joshua 24:15 says, "Choose this day whom you will serve." Was I
really serving just me?

I began to see that my walk with Christ needed a new defini-
tion—a complete soul surrender and wholehearted pursuit, putting
off things of me and putting on things of Him. I couldn't say no to
this call, couldn't wiggle out of it, and couldn't come up with any

excuse for why I shouldn't go exactly where He was directing me to go.

With my knees shaking and my heart quaking, I timidly answered the call to something bigger than myself, beyond my comfortable, easy-peasy, narrow-minded, college-y dreams and my safe little version of what the Christian life should look like. What I found in New York was an adventure chock-full of amazing, messy, hurting people. People like you and me. People who would change my heart and my viewpoint about God forever.

There in that thick humid air of the city, I knew for the first time in my life that I was exactly where I was supposed to be. It felt crazy and freeing and altogether wonderful. Like being inside a snow globe and someone suddenly turning you upside down. It was dirty, and hard, and pushed my comfort levels to their very limits, but it stretched me in all the right ways, ridding me of the biggest obstacle that stood in my path of growing in my walk with the Lord: me.

What I didn't expect was the beautiful friendships that would be established—the kind of relationships that don't waste time with surface niceties but dig right into the heart of a matter, diving in with the meat of God's Word and a richness only gained by a bold walk with Him. In fact, I'm still in contact with some of these soulful buddies, brothers and sisters who love God and love His people with a fierceness that challenges and encourages me. Folks who don't just talk about their faith but live it out in the everyday.

I wish I could say that from that day forward I have pursued Christ unswervingly and without a single hiccup, but that wouldn't be honest. And I'm a little afraid of lightning suddenly coming down from heaven and burning my self-serving heart to a crisp.

Now, granted, sometimes callings aren't so clear. Sometimes a calling means staying rather than going, or embracing and inviting in bravery where fear once dared to walk. A pursuing of God's righteousness over our right-ness, because right relationship is worth it. To leave our hands open to God's leading rather than squeezing our fists tight. It's giving Him full control and full rein of our future and future plans. And that's not exactly something that gives us the warm fuzzy feelings. In fact, sometimes, it's downright scary.

Matthew 5:23-24 talks about this kind of heart quandary, this opting to do what's right—even when ritual or outside forces press us to do differently. The willingness to leave the gift at the altar, if need be. It says, "If you are offering your gift at the altar and there remember that your brother has something against you, leave your gift there before the altar and go. First be reconciled to your brother, and then come and offer your gift."

This is a line drawn in the sand, a decision defined by steadfastness and surrender. A stretching act of obedience. A shaping. A pruning. A sculpting of character. One more way of choosing what's important.

The crazy thing is, sometimes what we're leaving behind may look good, like ministry or even worship. It may appear on the outside to be fueled by righteous desire and moral uprightness.

But maybe He's leading us to something more.

And so we seek. His good versus our own, His way over our will, His glory and His kingdom, first and foremost. Not because it's easy, but because His omniscience trumps our plans every time.

All the Good Things

The Important and Everything Else

To Remember

- Discipline is a learned skill, one we must practice to improve.
- Eternal things draw us closer while temporary things can draw us away.
- It's imperative we find a way around what hijacks our minds, because what we want most is waiting.
- Find those moments that matter and then make those moments a reality.

To Hold On To

Look carefully then how you walk, not as unwise but as wise, making the best use of the time, because the days are evil. Therefore do not be foolish, but understand what the will of the Lord is (Ephesians 5:15-17).

Seek first the kingdom of God and his righteousness (Matthew 6:33).

Choose this day whom you will serve (Joshua 24:15).

To Consider

Think of one thing that's weighing you down and causing you to lose perspective. Then ask yourself these two clarifying questions:

- Why does this matter to me today?
- Will it matter in a month? A year?

Part Four

All the People, All the Things

13

Too Busy for the Essentials

Amanda

*She generally gave herself very good advice
(though she very seldom followed it).*

LEWIS CARROLL, *ALICE'S ADVENTURES IN WONDERLAND*[1]

I die inside a little bit when people overly state the obvious.

For instance, when I'm in a store with all eight of my kids, I usually can't finish my shopping without fielding questions from people who find it hard to believe we're all one family. I answer,

"Yes, there are a lot of us."

"Yes, I'm here by myself with them."

"Yes, my hands are full. No, we are not a school on a field trip. No, I'm not brave, I'm their mom."

For the most part, this is just harmless and curious inquiry, and I don't mind it. I'm always kind to the onlookers, who are mostly kind as well. But I'd love for it to be okay that we're in the store just being us without every single time feeling like I'm leading a parade through the aisles.

Do people have to state the obvious? Like making comments to the pregnant woman with the large belly, the man with a limp, or the woman who's taller than most. These people already know what's different about them, right? Just this once she's hoping not to have a conversation about her size. He's tired of the limp being a thing for people. She feels like a circus act every time someone comments on her height.

Some things will always stand out to us, but we don't have to mention them.

Yet there's one glaringly obvious truth we all need to mention: We've made ourselves too busy for the essentials.

We've made ourselves too busy for the essentials.

Most of us can name our priorities. Way to go, us! But our real lives can look much different, as if we've allowed an unruly three-year-old to choose our priorities for us.

Eat.

Push for what we want.

Watch our favorite TV show.

Fight sleep.

This makes me laugh because it perfectly describes the preschoolers I've mothered.

We're good at naming our ideals, but what we do doesn't match our list or get us there. We lie in bed at night committed to doing better, but the next day we don't do it.

This is the story of my life. I wake up feeling horrible after eating too much sugar the day before, vowing to never do that again. Then the very next day I decide I didn't feel that bad after all, and I eat more of it. What I want for my health is thrown away in a hot second.

This is the story of my mom life too. I want to truly look my kids in the eye. I never want to make them wait while I'm doing something nonessential, like scrolling through and reading countless captions on social media I could look at after they're in bed. But I do make them wait, explaining that Mom's reading something. *Again.*

If my priority is looking at my children's faces and hearing what they have to say to me, then I must choose differently, right then, in that moment, not later. Author Greg McKeown put it this way:

> We overvalue nonessentials like a nicer car or house, or even intangibles like the number of our followers on Twitter or the way we look in our Facebook photos. As a result, we neglect activities that *are* truly essential, like spending time with our loved ones, or nurturing our spirit, or taking care of our health.[2]

It's like I tell my kids: "You won't be able to make a good choice just by thinking about it or even wanting it badly. Neither of those will make the move for you. You have to be the one to actually do it."

It's the same for us—we get to choose. That's both wonderful and terrifying.

Often when I'm overwhelmed by what's happening in my life, I open the journal I've set aside for "Things That Feel Too Hard" and write down every little detail about what, well, feels too hard. It's just a blank spiral-bound notebook I've trusted with my most honest pen scratches, and what I write is rarely in paragraph form. It's either a bunch of lists or short groupings of sentences touching on different areas that are taking up space in whatever part of the brain holds stressful stuff.

It becomes a brain dump of sorts.

Once I get my hardships written down, I feel so much better. I guess it's my version of laying down burdens. I pray through them before I close the front cover of my journal and set it back on the shelf, hoping to not have to pick it up for a while. Seeing my struggles and stressors laid out helps me see that what's been weighing me down *is* a lot. It would be a lot for anyone.

One thing that strikes me is that most of what I write about are

essentials: Family relationships. Struggling kids. Significant life circumstances. My big feelings.

I don't write about what I wore that day, how hot it is outside, or
how the humidity makes my hair look like one of those rope mops:
wet, stringy, and flat. What I write about ends up in this journal
because it's important to me. Important enough to fix.

It hangs so heavy because I care about it so much.

It's the same with the list of people and activities that make up our
lives. We get so frenzied in this great big juggle because we wonder
how we're going to do it all without mishandling or dropping one of
the items or people most meaningful to us. Regret about how we care-
lessly handled something or someone we care about stings, but the
opposite of this kind of regret is the freedom we have to decide what
we'll add to our schedules and lives.

We get to choose the essentials. We don't need to be juggling more
than we need to. Motherhood is busy, but it doesn't have to bury us.

14

Too Busy to Love

Amanda

There is no charm equal to tenderness of heart.

JANE AUSTEN, *EMMA*[1]

The ancient city of Ephesus, located in modern-day Turkey, was kind of like the New York City of the region. It was well populated, bustling, and politically influential. The Temple of Artemis, one of the Seven Wonders of the Ancient World, was also there.

Ephesus was known for its pagan superstition, worship of the goddess Diana, and for being religiously corrupt. But the church at Ephesus was alive and well—a strong church in Asia. The apostle Paul, who planted this church and lived among its members for three years, wrote the Bible's letter to the Ephesians he loved so much.

The apostle John, the author of Revelation, was one of Jesus's disciples and a prior church leader and resident of Ephesus. He received a vision of Jesus speaking to the key churches in Asia at the time. He gave a message to each one.

Revelation 2:1-7 reveals the message Jesus had for the church in Ephesus. In verse 1 He states His position of holding the church leaders in His right hand and how He walks among the churches—*so very near.*

Then in verses 2 and 3, Jesus mentions the good He sees them doing:

> "I know your works, your toil and your patient endurance, and how you cannot bear with those who are evil, but have tested those who call themselves apostles and are not, and found them to be false. I know you are enduring patiently and bearing up for my name's sake, and you have not grown weary."

He's saying they've persevered in their work as a church, called out the false teachers, and endured patiently for His name. They've not petered out, and He's proud of them. But wait, there's more. Something troubling is amid the good parts.

In verse 4, He says, "'But I have this against you, that you have abandoned the love you had at first.'"

The Ephesians got so busy doing good things that they forgot why they were doing them in the first place. They abandoned the flame of love they once had for Jesus and people, and it was showing.

As my pastor put it in a sermon about Ephesus, "One of the mistakes we make as believers is believing that busyness leads to godliness. Good things—even godly activities—can do great damage. Good things can easily distract us from the most important thing. The most important thing is love—love for Jesus and love for His people."[2]

They were so distracted by the course they were on that they missed the biggest thing: love.

None of what we involve ourselves in, our good motives aside, can replace relationship with and love for Jesus and people.

What motivates how we build our schedules? Is it relationship with Jesus and the people around us, or something else?

What strikes me about what currently fills my hours and days is that I haven't signed up to do anything other than what's necessary right now. I'm not volunteering at church, I'm not on any committees, and none of our kids will be involved in any extracurricular activities until our all-consuming family pace eases.

The only activities on my list are the non-negotiables: My relationship with God. Marriage. Mothering. Home. Church. Part-time work. School. Remodeling our house. Youth group for the teens and small group for us adults.

When you list them like that, they don't seem like much. But when you're living the list, it has the potential to flatten you—even when non-negotiables are the only things listed. Case in point:

- Marriage takes intentionality and lots of hard work.

- Mothering my crew is insanely hard sometimes. The special needs and sheer number of children are a great responsibility.

- A home can't run itself, and people need to eat and wear clothes.

- Attending church is a highlight of our week, and getting out the door on time with everyone in non-pajamas is quite a feat.

- Part-time work (though partly done from home) pulls in ways I can't always relieve. I can't just stop everything and complete my work whenever I want to.

- Homeschooling half our crew all day long and evenings filled with public school homework for the other half is intense.

- Remodeling a home is grueling with a work crew of 80 percent children. Lord willing, by the time this book goes to print, we'll be finished renovating and enjoying our home on the creek. But right now, it's such a mess.

- Youth group and small group take time, but they keep us outside our bubble. (We need this so much.)

When you're living the list, it has the potential to flatten you.

That's a pretty lengthy list of non-negotiables. Some things we just can't let go. Even when you're overwhelmed by busyness, you have core responsibilities that must be attended.

Amid all these must-dos, however, we can't lose ourselves. We serve and pour ourselves out for the sake of others, yes, but not to the point of losing ourselves. When our souls get so backed up that we're not doing anything well, it's time to gather ourselves. Sometimes that means cutting our activities even further, right down to the barest of bones.

When our souls get so backed up that we're not doing anything well, it's time to gather ourselves.

We're paring down, so we can build back up. We're making sure we're still functioning as we're intended to. The question is this: Do we want to be too busy for what is most important to us?

What do the absolute necessities look like for us and our lives? Are the activities we've added to our lives helping or hurting? Are they truly as vital as we claim? Or are we processing our lives and schedules while looking through an unhealthy lens?

Since the necessities alone are so, so much work, shouldn't we give them our best?

Distracted by Everyone and Everything

Anne-Renee

We won't be distracted by comparison if we are captivated by purpose.

Bob Goff[1]

I watched them go by, one by one. Gorgeously groomed mamas on parade, waltzing into the coffee shop where I was hiding and hoping against hope that my Move to Alaska To-Do List would miraculously disappear while I was sipping on a delicious latte.

No such luck.

Each woman was carrying a designer diaper bag, an expensive eco-friendly purse, and an eye-cringingly bright bleached smile. They pushed strollers worth three digits plus, with quiet, sleeping little cherubs all decked out in trendy babywear and coordinating blanket sets.

I instinctively sank my body further down into my seat, suddenly aware of my stretched-out leftover maternity jeans and snot-encrusted sweater.

My mind immediately started working out an equation: me versus them.

Me: tired and frumpy

Them: bright-eyed and put together

Me: hanging by a thread

Them: perfect bodies draped in stylish threads

Me: wanting to wipe the floor with their glowing, sickeningly sweet smiles

Them: clueless to my existence

Sometimes the biggest distractions aren't devices or flashing lights or discontented dreams, but living, breathing people.

Comparison, as the saying goes, is the thief of joy. And not only is comparison a dirty rotten thief, but it's a spoiler that can suddenly become an obsession—one that damages gratification and destroys gladness of heart.

The crazy thing is, most days, comparison comes to us as effortlessly as breathing. It's just so easy to look around at what everyone else is doing, or wearing, or being, and allow ourselves to drown in a pool of compare and contrast and me versus them. It's a dangerous trap that can jump up and grab at a tired mama mind faster than you can say *social media*—draining her of all joy and peace and contentment.

We can so quickly become fixated on how others are doing life: baby showers, birth plans, monthly photo posts with the appropriate number fastened on their little cutie's chest. First words, first tooth, first steps, first birthday, first Christmas, first day of school. First concert, first prom, first car. First wedding and first grandchild.

We begin to think our lives should mirror those around us. Because what if we're not doing this mothering thing right? What if everyone else is doing it better? And what if we can't keep up?

It's like we're all on this giant mothering racetrack with each mom assigned to a different lane. But as the gun goes off and the race begins, we notice some moms aren't even running. Some are riding brand-new bicycles and passing us so quickly they almost appear to be a roadrunner-ish blur. Others seem to have left the track and are doing stretches and cool-down exercises, as though they've already completed the race.

Then much to our chagrin we realize most of the other participants are wearing a whole different line of running gear than we are, clearly more lightweight with brighter colors and flashier fabrics. It's way better than our embarrassing post-maternity getup.

In that moment, our confidence pops like a balloon in a humid car on a hot, sticky summer day. Suddenly our dingy old workout attire and plain gray Nikes don't seem all that wonderful. Maybe they're even slowing us down.

Instead of concentrating on staying in our own mothering lane, we look at all the other lanes—and even outside the lanes—distracted by everything and everyone, desperately trying to fit our stride and appearance into a certain mold.

We put such stock in what others believe and feel that we can readily turn to people pleasing rather than to God pleasing, focusing on how everyone else is doing life rather than how God is calling us to do life. That, of course, affects everything—how we view our bodies, our homes, our cars, our marriages, our families, our mothering, our callings. And not in a good way.

Then there's the other side of comparison, which is equally destructive. The side that likes to soothe and console with thoughts like *I'm so much better in this area than she is because I do it this way*, which of course would be the right way. *Oh, poor Anna. She just can't quite get the knack of how to juggle a playdate, naptime, and preparing dinner for her family in a single day. Clearly having that fourth child has been way too much for her. Bless her little heart.*

This kind of detrimental thinking tears others down in order to boost ourselves up. It's a comforting kind of comparison, a bandage for insecurity and a pacifying nightcap for the desperate and lonely.

It's like the two sides of a teeter-totter. The more the side we're not on is pushed toward the ground, the higher we fly up-up-up toward the sky. And you've got to admit, it kind of feels good. Or at least it does for a little while. It cloaks and calms our questioning souls like nothing else can, covering uncertainty with a blanket of confident assurance, letting us know that, yes indeed, we're doing life the right way. Those other moms just haven't quite figured it out yet. Poor souls.

Sadly, sometimes we've been at this comparison game for so long that we're no longer sure what we personally like or feel or want. We've filled our minds and hearts to overflowing with the thoughts and reflections of others, and now we're uncertain of who we are and what makes us tick.

Sometimes we allow our identity to be shaped by the images of those around us to such an extent that we no longer feel confident in who God created us to be. Our gifts and talents are pushed back in favor of what others are doing, while the manifestations of our distinct personality become buried in the muck of uniformity's murky waters.

Who are we? And why can't we seem to focus on just one way of doing life?

Maybe it's time to let go, to slough off those mental measurements and critiques, those joy robbers. To remember and revive the remarkable women God created us to be. To take time to unearth what He has for us in this amazing world, and to find our glorious place in it.

Because, praise God, He has so much more planned for us!

He's crafted each of us with unique, pulsating desires, personalities, and bents all our own. We're not cookie cutter replications of one another but glorious reflections of the Creator. Who we are is already set. He "chose us in him before the foundation of the world" (Ephesians 1:4). Let me say that again: *He* chose *us*! The plans He has for us were set into motion long before we were even born. In the words of Jeremiah 29:11, "I know the plans I have for you, declares the LORD, plans for welfare and not for evil, to give you a future and a hope."

He has good plans. For us. *All* of us!

Imagine if we were to pour all our energies into the life God has given us, bringing it all before Him as we seek to do His will in our individual walks and families. What if we stopped looking to the left or to the right, but instead looked solely at Him? What if we focused on how He wants us to walk and breathe and live and mother, and not how anyone else is doing it? For when we seek to know God better, we also learn to know ourselves better, getting back to who He created us to be. Instead of focusing on how everyone else is doing life, we can simply focus on how He wants us to do life.

When it comes down to it, we have only one opportunity here on earth to do this living life thing well. Tomorrow can't be rushed, and today will never come again, so let's make each moment count. This one life is *our* one life. We don't get a second chance.

What a perspective changer! Living for Him versus living for others. What a liberating life that would be—to make decisions based on His words and no one else's. To seek His face to determine what to do and think and feel and be, rather than looking to the faces of those around us.

What peace. What purpose. What freedom!

So why are we letting other people and other things stand in our way?

Frederick Buechner wrote,

> Stop trying to protect, to rescue, to judge, to manage the lives around you—your children's lives, the lives of your husband, your wife, your friends—because that is just what you are powerless to do. Remember that the lives of other people are not your business. They are

their business. They are God's business because they all have God whether they use the word God or not. Even your own life is not your business. It also is God's business. Leave it to God. It is an astonishing thought. It can become a life-transforming thought.[2]

16

When Comparison Is a Good Thing

Anne-Renee

*The first great and primary business to which I ought to attend
every day was, to have my soul happy in the Lord.*

George Müller[1]

flipped through the pages of my Bible feeling exasperated and, frankly, fried. I felt like this book held so many rules, had so many conditions, and highlighted so many ways I didn't measure up.

You see, I'm way too quick to judge others, render harsh phrases to my kids when kind ones are needed, and withhold forgiveness and grace when compassionate love needs to have the final word.

Plus, I stink at having a regular time in the Word. I'll start a Bible study, and halfway through I'll be distracted and give up, never finishing. And don't get me started on prayer time. Half the time I fall asleep or start thinking about something totally random, like what we need at the grocery store or a song from a movie we just saw. My brain is like a pinball machine way before it's time to say *amen*.

As I sat praying about all these swirling feelings and processing my noticeable unworthiness, I was struck yet again by my smallness in contrast to God's blatant bigness, my little life against His mighty vastness, and my itty-bitty place in His great wide world.

I'd been trying so hard not to compare myself to others that I had mistakenly assumed all comparison is bad. I was fully aware of the yuck within me, but desired to be more like Him: full of love, joy, peace, patience, kindness, goodness, faithfulness, gentleness, and what seemed like the holy grail of all Christian character qualities, self-control. It dawned on me that these attributes were fruits of the Spirit, produced only by walking in the Spirit and being led by the Spirit (Galatians 5:16-26). So I started writing down what I know God to be: faithful, majestic, unchanging, wise, all-powerful, all-knowing, ever-present, compassionate, holy, just, righteous, true to His word, merciful, forgiving, sovereign, and full of love.

Then I made a list of all the things He's done, both for us as His children, and for me specifically.

Last, I wrote down promises He's made through the years, for all of us.

And something incredible happened. The more I focused on God, rather than fixating on myself, the more and more His presence enveloped my soul, shrouding my worries and fears and speaking life into the hurting places. It was as if an ocean of love overcame me. A flooding of His peace. A calmness covered me, seeping down into the questioning corners of uncertainty.

All I could whisper in that moment was, "Make me like You, Lord. Please make me like You."

It's not that I want to be God. No, no. Far from it. I don't want the position of holding the world in place or the role of refereeing the nations. But I do want to make much of God, using all that I do, all that I am, and anything that might amaze or make a difference in this troubled world to turn eyes back to the Creator.

I want to echo David's words in saying, "Create in me a clean heart,

O God" (Psalm 51:10). I want my heart to become more and more like His heart, my thoughts like His thoughts, my responses more in line with His.

Goodness knows, there are plenty of days I completely blow it and gush my aggravation and bad attitude onto my husband and kiddos and anyone else in my path. But that's when I'm reminded how much I need God. Oh, how I need Him!

I need Him to surgically remove all the nasty, sinful plaque coating the interior of my heart and replace it with His tender heart. Infusing me with compassion and a love for those around me. Giving me a love for the lost, a faith that can move mountains, and the desire to follow hard after Him.

This is not a striving for perfection or even self-improvement, for we know we can't be perfect this side of heaven. But we can endeavor to grow in Him, to dig deep into His Word, and to seek first His kingdom and His righteousness. This is more than merely trying to be good or striving to do the right thing, more than memorizing verses and checking spiritual boxes. This is a matter of letting Him be Lord over all, giving Him VIP access to every part of our being.

So often I think our Christian culture, though perhaps unintentionally, puts such an emphasis on keeping our character and reputation squeaky clean that we forget it's really about obedience, love for our Lord, and being willing to follow Him no matter what. Because sometimes following Jesus is a little messy. Dirty, even. But we don't like to talk about that part of discipleship. Just thinking about it makes us want to squirm in our comfy Christian seats, while unconsciously dusting off our Sunday best.

We become distracted by following the rules rather than focused on following the Ruler of all. But the rules are just a guideline of love from a loving Father. Because of the cross, because when "the Son sets you free, you will be free indeed" (John 8:36), we are free to wholeheartedly follow Him.

The thing is, I can't ignore my sin. Nor do I want to diminish the amazing work Christ is doing in me, because of His love, because of His mercy, because of His sacrifice at Calvary. For the cross changes everything—my past, my present, my future. It wrecks my pride, my selfishness, and my desire for gain and conquest.

The cross changes everything—my past, my present, my future.

As I proclaim Jesus as Lord of my life and yearn to live in alignment with Him, I begin to see the transformation the Holy Spirit is doing around me and in me. In the quietness. In the craziness. In the unexpected. With this soulful makeover, I begin to see myself as He sees me—a beautifully broken child of the King, bought with the precious blood of Christ, the Lamb, the Son of God. Through this glorious lens of grace, I am clean. I am a holy, beloved daughter, a legitimate heir to the throne. My salvation is firm, and my way is set.

The best compliment in the world would be for someone to say I remind them of Christ. If I do, it's because Christ is in me! And His presence alters everything.

The apostle Paul put it this way: "Be imitators of me, as I am of Christ" (1 Corinthians 11:1). Paul was acknowledging that any good he accomplished had been for bringing others to Christ, not for his own gain. For those applauding his efforts, he simply pointed them back to the source of it all: the one and only begotten Son of God, Jesus.

Comparison doesn't always have to be bad. Comparing ourselves to God and desiring to be more like Him can be a powerful reminder of our unworthiness in light of His holiness, a beautiful remembrance of His prevailing sacrifice, and the perfect mirror for a forgetful daughter who wants to mirror her Father in all things. He is our firm foundation, the Rock of Ages upon which our hope is built. Yes, as His children, we do have a holy responsibility to reflect our Father in an accurate, loving, responsive way. To reveal to an aching world just who God is and to share the saving power of His Son. I mean, we can't just be selfish and keep all this goodness to ourselves. Rather, we are called to bring hope to the hurting and truth to the searching, and to extend His grace and reveal His heart to the lost.

We are called to be the gospel in action.

Answering this call isn't about a list of dos and don'ts and doing whatever it takes to achieve perfection. Most days it will probably look rather muddled, messy, and imperfect. But it's part of the Great Commission. The going forth. The doing. The telling. The sharing. Not because we're all that, but because He is. And that makes all the difference.

Maybe it's time to exchange our exasperations for prayerful utterances. Maybe something a little like this:

> *Father God, thank You for who You are, for Your unfailing love and extraordinary sacrifice. You are the ultimate example of what love is all about. We fall short so often. Please forgive us. We want to follow You, to walk in Your ways and Your truth. Pry us from our comfort zones and positions of complacency. Move us into Your will, alongside Your heart, so we can serve You with an active, obedient, compassionate love. Make us like You, we pray. In Jesus's name, amen.*

All the Good Things

All the People, All the Things

To Remember

- Motherhood is busy, but it doesn't have to bury us.
- What we involve ourselves in can't replace our love for Jesus and people.
- Tomorrow can't be rushed, and today will never come again, so let's make each moment count.
- The cross changes everything—our past, our present, our future.

To Hold On To

Faith, hope, and love abide, these three; but the greatest of these is love (1 Corinthians 13:13).

The fruit of the Spirit is love, joy, peace, patience, kindness, goodness, faithfulness, gentleness, self-control; against such things there is no law. And those who belong to Christ Jesus have crucified the flesh with its passions and desires. If we live by the Spirit, let us also keep in step with the Spirit (Galatians 5:22-25).

To Consider

Read Galatians 5:22-25 above.

- What is one fruit of the Spirit you can focus on this week in your interactions with the people in your life?

Part Five

Not Yets and Daydreams

17

Our Regular Life Is Just So Much

Amanda

But I suppose there might be good in things, even if we don't see it.

Frances Hodgson Burnett[1]

We were married on an 83-degree day in Alaska during the summer of 1999. I mention the temperature only because it was quite the anomaly. Alaskans can generally count the number of truly hot days in a year on one hand. Even in summer, a coolness is in the air most days.

Despite the heat, our wedding was fun, and being married was a relief after four years of college dating. Like many couples, we had a "plan" for when we wanted to start a family. Two years seemed like a sensible time to wait, so we went with that.

Feel free to ask me how that went.

I'd laugh and tell you we celebrated our first anniversary the following summer with a camping trip in the mountains and me five months pregnant, sleeping on a tent floor padded with gravel. Our first son was born four months later, and the babies kept coming after that. The first three children—the only ones we thought we'd ever have—arrived in 2000, 2002, and 2004. Two boys and a girl. Boom, boom, boom.

Our informal "routine" had been to welcome a baby approximately every two years, and when we passed that mark after our third, I became a little antsy. What should we do? Were we done? We prayed hard and long about a fourth child; it felt monumental to consider another. Drew, Gavin, and Morgan kept me super busy, and I loved being their mama. Admittedly, I was a bit afraid to mess with what we already had going. We had our fair share of toddler and baby mayhem, for sure, including a three-year-old who refused to open his mouth and eat at dinnertime, but our life felt safe-ish and sort of predictable.

One morning I was standing in a hot hotel shower in Nashville, three thousand miles from home and praying about whether we should try for that fourth baby. I was attending a conference with five thousand other mothers of preschoolers. I don't know if it was the baby fever hanging around the conference center or that a whole lot of estrogen and pregnant bellies were flowing in that place, but my mind was in a mess.

Just as I started praying in that shower, I looked down at my stomach. And there, as plain as day and somehow shaped by hot water that pulled my blood to the surface of my skin, was a perfectly tied pink bow, right over my womb. I'm not even kidding. I can see it now. I was so astounded that when I got myself together and came out of the bathroom, I drew a picture for my roommates. This sign was just so blatant.

I wasn't pregnant yet, but I knew right then that children were a gift and we were meant to have another.

A chubby-cheeked baby girl was born to us 17 months later, and we named her Annika. That was in 2008, and since then we've welcomed four more children, three through adoption and one more by birth. I crack up at us agonizing about a fourth child. If I'd known then about the fifth, sixth, seventh, and eighth we'd also parent in the near future, I would have been doing a lot more than agonizing. Brown paper bags would have been involved, and probably some valium too.

Our life is plain crazy. If you need convincing, get this: our kids were born in 2000, 2002, 2004, 2007, 2008, 2010, 2010, and 2012. *Oh my stars. What has happened?*

It's been so hard to do anything exciting for myself, because my life has been completely and utterly wild for nearly two decades now. My "fun" has turned into showering and picking out clothes for myself for the next day. *Whoop-de-doo.* I know how to have a good time.

Because this has been my life (let's throw in that I homeschooled all my kids exclusively for the first decade, and then half of them for the last three years), I'd say I know a thing or two about having desires I cannot act on. My regular life with no add-ins is just so much.

We probably don't share the same family dynamics, but I'm pretty sure you, as a mom, can say the same. We're unfortunate experts at longing for what we can't quite have or attain, because our regular lives are already just so much.

Did I mention we've added a puppy to the family? It makes me laugh and shake my head, because we always seem to be operating at some level of insanity.

In all seriousness, what happens when we long for something so hard and for so long that we act on it whenever we feel like it instead of waiting for the proper time? We're so distracted by our desires (which aren't all bad) that we get tunnel vision and can't see what's truly good for us and our families in a certain window of time.

I often talk to my kids about the boundaries they're not real excited about, yet need to live within. For instance, they might be unhappy about their bedtime, a privilege that was removed, or how an older sibling has more freedom than they do. I'll say, "Try to remember the limitations in your life are good for you instead of out to get you."

Each time I say that out loud to one of them, it penetrates deep within my own heart. Do I believe my current limitations are a benefit to me? I can't say that's always the case.

If our lives are already full, with no extras added in, shouldn't that tell us something? Sometimes I miss what my situation is trying to tell me: I have all I need. Everything God has given me to do so far is already right in front of me, and the people He's given me to love are here too. Now it's up to me how I respond to my life, how I care for what I've already been given. We may not be able to do everything we want to do, so how about we decide to want what we already have? After all, today is the only day we're promised.

I love the way Elisabeth Elliot says it: "The life of faith is lived one day at a time, and it has to be *lived*—not always looked forward to as though the 'real' living were around the next corner. It is today for which we are responsible. God still owns tomorrow."[2]

What we hope for in the future isn't yet ours. What we've already been given is right here, waiting to be wanted.

18

Untimely Desires

Amanda

*God will either give us what we ask or give us what we would
have asked if we knew everything he knows.*

TIMOTHY KELLER[1]

Ten years ago I joined a gym. Monumental, huh?

It was a cool place for women to work out. A gal from my hometown opened it after leaving Alaska for college and coming back with a physique any woman would die for. She was a hardcore personal trainer, but her methods produced amazing results, and she was such a cheerleader for the women who came through her doors. Plus, she offered free childcare in the next room.

Win. Sold. I'm in.

I took the free class she offered to curious onlookers and decided it was just the kick in the pants I needed to get my health on track again after our fourth little one was born. For four months I dragged my troops up the narrow steps and into their class, and for four months I cycled, lifted, and kickboxed my way to feeling better about myself and my health.

Then my real life hit me.

An old injury from a car accident I was in at age 16 flared while I was lying on my back doing an exercise, and just like that I was out of the game. I could no longer do any of the moves, and I had to quit. Imagine the saddest, most downtrodden woman who was finally getting her life back, only to have it ripped from her. That was me.

I was heartbroken. I'd finally returned to feeling like the athlete I'd been, and then this happened. I missed that part of me, the part that felt strong and energetic. I also loved what I was showing my kids, that healthy people care for their bodies by moving them.

For the ten years that followed that fateful day in class, and up until this very moment, I've been unable to exercise. My injury flares each time I do, and it depresses me. I've been tempted to shout at heaven about it, but instead I try again and again, making this adjustment or trying that method, to no avail.

It's just not my time. I don't know if I'll ever understand it.

Yet everyone has lived with the ache of untimely desires, those longings unfulfilled because it's not the right time. I think all of creation groans with us on this one.

I know my sad story is a bit depressing because we moms are already sensitive about what we can and can't do in this stage of life. But my point is this: Our desires are important, and we must keep them alive, but they aren't always fit for acting on right now.

It doesn't seem fair to have to sit on the sidelines for something so good (like a desire to exercise or work at a business or a hobby) while we slave away at this motherhood gig we can't just set aside no matter how we feel. I don't think it's that we're sad that it's unfair. I think we're sad because we just want to be us again.

We don't think it's too much to ask. We just didn't realize motherhood would be so wonderful and all-consuming all at once. We didn't know we'd have so many unfulfilled desires. My desire to be physically fit again wasn't unhealthy, but my thoughts about my inability to be that person were.

God, I prayed, *why did You bring me this far to have me pour myself out over and over and never get filled back up? Am I going to continue to feel like my body is wasting away while it takes my mind with it?*

As I read the pages of Scripture, God reminds me, *I'm the One who fills. I made you to pour yourself out. When you do, you're following Jesus's example.*

I ask him, *God, will I ever get to live out the dreams I have or the visions You've placed in me for the future?"*

Again, He urges, *What if* I *were your dream? What if* I *were your future? Because I am. Let me handle the timing of things. Rest in where you are right now, sweet girl.*

I don't know if the sweeping crescendo of the inspirational instrumental music I'm listening to is to blame or not, but as I typed what God might say back when we ask our questions, I got all choked up.

He *is* the One who fills. He *is* our dream. Isn't He?

Maybe His dream for us now is different from what we think it should be. Are we pushing against what needs to be happening in our lives in this season in favor of grumping our way through because our days don't look like we hoped they would? I know I have. My family knows it too.

Sometimes I have to come to a full stop, usually when I'm in the car by myself (oh so rare) and have some time to really think. I realize I'm about to lose it, but I don't want to. I park and, resting my hands on my legs, then turning my relaxed palms upward, I pray, *Show me the way to go, Lord. Show me the way to be. I can't go on like this.*

The angst burns me up. The dissatisfaction with how I've been acting and thinking overwhelms me. I must change, and I know it's my choice. My circumstances are never guaranteed to change, especially in my favored way or in my perfect timeline. The only thing I can change is me—my attitude, my outlook, and choosing where I look for guidance.

My healthy desires are *good*. My being in a funk about the timing of them is not.

My healthy desires are *good*. My being in a funk about the timing of them is not.

19

What the Daydreams Won't Tell You

Anne-Renee

Keep your heart with all vigilance, for from it flow the springs of life.
PROVERBS 4:23

S omething happens to our mental state when we start a family. Yes, we can all nod our heads and chuckle at this, because we know it to be true. We've seen it and experienced it firsthand. The reality is that our minds get quite the workout with added tasks and additional people to take care of.

But this is about more than just a forgetfulness or brain overload. This is a replacement of sorts. A perfectly synchronized swap of who we used to be (that girl who spent her weekends running fun little errands and meeting a friend for coffee) for the juggling wonder mom. She's also known as the human tissue, referee, family nurse, chief comforter, chef in charge, household logistics coordinator, hazmat cleanup supervisor, and scheduling queen.

This is a substitution procedure of sorts, replacing contentment in our current situation with a prickling curiosity in the form of a nagging question: *Who might I have been had children not become a part of my everyday reality?*

Alongside the tiredness, frustration, and everyday wear and tear on a mama's body and brain, self-loathing can creep in. Like a Buy One, Get One kind of deal, the deeper we get into motherhood, the bigger the mountains of doubt and dislike often become. We can't seem to help this loving and loathing, *loving* them while *loathing* what our lives have become. Who *we* have become.

We fail to see that Dissatisfaction is a cousin to Distraction.

Maybe it's an aging thing as well. The older we get, the harder we fight to like ourselves. Gray hairs, wrinkles, and fatigue arrive unbidden. We feel a lack of the zest and gusto that defined our younger years.

And yet looking at a toddler making faces at himself in a mirror is all it takes to begin to remember. The carefreeness of whirling and twirling. The giddiness that bubbles up when playing dress up or flying a toy airplane. The sheer delight at the sight of balloons, trains, fireworks, or animals at the zoo. We reflect on when we were free with our emotions, living with unbridled pleasure and unhindered joy.

Before all the responsibilities. Before all the lists. Before all the people.

Sometimes this looking back can be good and productive. Other times it just makes us sad and discontented. We begin to compare our lives now to our lives then, a BC/AC point of view: Before Children and After Children.

Most of the time these thoughts or diversions seem harmless; we don't even realize their danger or potential to harm. But with a little encouragement, a little watering, these tiny, seemingly innocent seeds of unhappiness begin to sink into our souls, making us irritated mamas desiring change. As Elisabeth Elliot warned, "The secret is Christ in me, not me in a different set of circumstances."[1]

There's something so powerful about discontentment. Those *What-if* questions and *If-only* daydreams can change the thermostat of a marriage or alter a mom's desire to nurture and serve her family, amending plans for the future and throwing the whole family into a state of disarray. If not held in check, those daydreams can multiply oh so quickly, taking over our thought processes, our desires, and finally, our actions before we even realize what's happening. They begin to color how we view the world and what's going on around us, painting glorious pictures of what could be and what might have been.

Maybe this seed of discontent starts with a remembering, with recalling that first love or first kiss, the kind that makes a married woman read old love letters or dig through mementos from her past. Or a private conversation with an old flame on social media that leads to an undercurrent of giddiness when a new message arrives. What may begin as a fun, meaningless friendship that makes you smile and feel appreciated can quickly turn into something more.

I've watched families near and dear to me fall apart over what started as a little twinge of restlessness, of wishing life could be a little different.

This is not something to play with, friends. I'm convinced beyond a shadow of a doubt that the Enemy would love nothing better than for us to question God's goodness to us in the here and in the now. For us to forget how blessed we are. For us to wonder whether something better might be out there for us.

Again, having seen this personally, I can tell you that what you think could be better is not going to be better. Most likely there will be scars and emotional repercussions for years to come if we allow these daring daydreams. But you can't understand the aftermath or ramifications if you don't fully understand the dangerous weapon you're playing with.

Several years ago, I noticed this trend among married moms of joking about hot hubbies. Not talking about their own husbands, mind you, but which celebrities would be their dream husbands. Some women even established their Top Five. As in five celebrities they'd ditch their husbands for.

What started as a joke materialized into something more for some of the couples. The kind of more that rips apart a family and causes generational havoc. Eyes that were once glued onto their own families and marriages were now fixed on the door of possibility, of what else, or who else, might be out there. My husband and I watched as families around us began to fall apart. And not just one family, but several families within our circle of friends. Families that had once been rooted in biblical truth.

Now, not all dreams are bad. No, no. Quite the opposite. In fact, God often spoke to His people in biblical times utilizing dreams and visions. Think of Abraham. Jacob. Joseph. Pharaoh. Solomon. Daniel. John the Baptist's father, Zechariah. Jesus's earthly father, Joseph. Peter. Paul. And John. These dreams have been recorded and copied for centuries. Evidence of God desiring to communicate with His people. But that's not the kind of dreams we're talking about here.

Unhindered daydreams can be dangerous if allowed to grow. If not properly aligned with Scripture to hold them accountable or prayed over with godly friends to help keep them in check, these seemingly harmless dreams can turn into a woman's worst nightmare. I don't know how many times I've caught myself soaking in a tub of dissatisfaction over where we currently live. I love Alaska, I do. Well, okay, *most* of the time I love Alaska. But occasionally I catch myself daydreaming about living somewhere that doesn't define downtown shopping as a one-stop-shop strip mall with sushi, tax service, a smoke shop, IT repair, alterations, a barbershop, a liquor store, and a quickie mart all in the same place. Where local restaurant reviews don't include phrases like, "surprisingly decent," "typical fare," and "pretty good…for Alaska."

A hidden place deep down inside me really wants to live somewhere *chichi*. That word alone shouts elegance and sophistication, a place containing all the niceties city living offers, with buildings taller than three stories and overflowing with good restaurants, museums, theaters, parks, playgrounds, boutiques, quaint bakeries, and cozy coffee shops.

In the first ten years of living here, I had to be ultra-vigilant about letting those inner grumblings turn into outward actions. Loud mental complaining became my forte. Anytime I felt that claustrophobic cloud hanging over my head, the one that made me feel antsy and discontent with where we lived, I had to remind myself that God put me here for a reason, that His plans were better than mine, and that He could see things I couldn't.

Honestly, some days I still have to do this, because my mind is forgetful and my emotions are fickle. *I love Alaska. I hate Alaska. I love Alaska.* I have to work to see the beauty around me. And oh my goodness, there sure is a lot of beauty stored up here in this glorious state. But it requires removing the selfish blinders I've allowed to surround my discontented eyes, keeping them trained on the place God wants me to be. At least for now.

We need to beware. To be vigilant. To take our thoughts and ponderings seriously. Second Corinthians 10:5 warns us to "take every thought captive," making them obedient to Christ. If we want to focus on what's truly important, we have to decide what in the world to do with this lack of love for ourselves and our present circumstances. We need to say no to the distraction of detrimental daydreams and keep our hearts and minds focused on the Lord and on what He has for us and our families. To discipline our thoughts and *What-if* questions and replace them with God's truth—who He is, what He has done, and what He will do.

Maybe that means turning those daydreams into prayers, laying our hopes and dreams at His feet and trusting Him to help us wade through them. Or maybe that simply means doing the next good thing, keeping our heads out of the clouds and focusing on what God has placed right in front of us, like loving our families and loving them well.

Perhaps the next time we're struggling with discontentment or the desire to look elsewhere for comfort, this verse will help: "Let the words of my mouth and the meditation of my heart be acceptable in your sight, O LORD, my rock and my redeemer" (Psalm 19:14). In this psalm we see a way to check ourselves as we seek what God has for us, as we pursue what will draw us closer to Him and align our desires and dreams with His.

And if He says it's good, then it's good.

20

The Uncomfortable Wait

Anne-Renee

I wait for the LORD, my soul waits.

PSALM 130:5

How long, O LORD? Will you forget me forever? How long will you hide your face from me? How long must I take counsel in my soul and have sorrow in my heart all the day? How long shall my enemy be exalted over me?

PSALM 13:1-2

Wait for the LORD; be strong, and let your heart take courage; wait for the LORD!

PSALM 27:14

Patience and I are not exactly what you would call the best of friends. I hate waiting, whether in a doctor's office, a grocery store checkout line, or during the longest nine months of your life, also known as pregnancy.

When I was expecting my daughter, Kailee, the midwives told me that, based on my health, my size, my cervix, and the size and development of the baby, I would probably deliver around two weeks before my due date, give or take a day or two. As that time drew closer, I was ecstatic. I couldn't wait to meet my darling baby girl.

The days seemed to creep by. *Finally*, it was two weeks before my due date, but my chance of going into labor was zilch. Nada. Nothing was going on in the southern regions of my body except extreme discomfort.

Then one week before my due date arrived. At sloth speed, mind you. And as the midwives checked and poked and probed, they discovered my little lamb was posterior. Somehow my sweet babe had gotten her position all mixed up and was now pushing on my back and my spine, making moving and breathing, and living in general, quite uncomfortable.

We started a long list of things to encourage our girl to turn around the proper direction. Certain exercises. Avoiding all reclining positions. Crawling around on my hands and knees. Homeopathic remedies. Baths. Sleeping on my left side. Chiropractic appointments. You name it, we tried it. As first-time parents, we were willing to do anything we were told, anything that would move the process along.

When I focused on the act of waiting itself, I was anxious. But when I disciplined myself to focus on the baby to come and prepare for her arrival, I could cope so much better.

At long last, five days *after* my due date, I went into labor. At this point, I was discouraged and sick of waiting. The baby still had not turned, and the pain in my back was the worst I'd ever experienced. If people had told me to wait on the Lord, I probably would have punched them in the face. But no one did. All they said was, "This too shall pass." Not exactly the encouraging words this first-time mama wanted to hear.

Thankfully, labor doesn't last forever (although it seems like it will at the time), and after 37 and a half hours, Kailee Renee Gumley made her much anticipated entrance into the world, chubby cheeked and full of dimples.

Suddenly, the waiting was forgotten. The pain was a dim memory. Here in our arms was *love*—boisterous, swollen-eyed, doughy warm love. Our hearts felt like they would explode, stretched to new heights as we held our exquisite, tiny bundle of joy.

Good thing I didn't know then that my son would arrive even later beyond his due date than his big sister had, as in ten days later. We dubbed him the Poky Little Puppy and the baby who needed an eviction notice to vacate the premises.

Waiting is hard. It's uncomfortable and goes against our on-demand culture. And yet think of the beauty of Advent, when we celebrate and remember the God-baby who came to earth two thousand years ago. The Israelites had dreamed about the expected Rescuer and triumphant Messiah to come. For years! Waiting. Waiting. Holding on to precious, prophesied threads of hope through the hardships of slavery and the horrors of wars, famine, kingdom upsets, and exile. Always looking to the future for the One who would make all things right. The One who, rather than making a majestic entrance and riding in on a royal chariot, arrived in startling childish form. Without pomp and circumstance. Without proper nursing staff or a germ-free delivery room. Without a kingly crown to grace His noble head.

But as believers who know how the story will end, we can rejoice in what was, soaking in the wonder of what is, while looking forward to what will be: His coming again.

We can rejoice in what was, soaking in the wonder of what is, while looking forward to what will be: His coming again.

The restlessness of this present state of waiting is minimized by the miracle and marvel of what is to come: a creation forever good. A new heaven and a new earth, where God's dwelling place will be amid His children. Where "they will be his people, and God himself will be with them as their God. He will wipe away every tear from their eyes, and death shall be no more, neither shall there be mourning, nor crying, nor pain anymore, for the former things have passed away" (Revelation 21:3-4).

This is one of those rare times when the waiting is not a distraction, but rather a glorious golden carrot at the end of a long laborious race. There's an incentive feeding our motivation. And our desire to utilize each day for the kingdom is only intensified by such remembering.

Then there's the waiting that seems to take forever (like pregnancy), overhauling our hearts and minds. The kind of waiting that takes over our body and all its senses, becoming the only thing we think about, talk about, and pray about.

Ben Patterson has said, "At least as important as the things we wait for is the work God wants to do in us as we wait."[1]

How can we shift our focus from the waiting itself into the realm of waiting well? Of believing well? Trusting that His timing is better than ours. Trusting that He sees all and knows all. Trusting that He has our good in mind. All. The. Time. So whether we are waiting for a baby, or a diagnosis, or reconciliation to a broken relationship, we can rest in His omniscience and His unshakable, unfailing love.

Maybe with those belated little babies of mine, God was putting together the perfect all-star hospital staff to help us through the birthing process. Maybe He wanted to bless someone else with our delivery experiences. Maybe He was simply stretching me. Those *maybes* can drive us crazy, multiplying anxiousness and magnifying fears, reminding us that we are not in control. And boy oh boy, do we like to be in control as human beings.

In Psalm 130, we find a writer desperate for forgiveness and calling out to God for mercy. What stands out to me in this poetic petition, however, isn't the pleas themselves, but how he waits with anticipation: "My soul waits for the Lord more than watchmen for the morning" (verse 6). This isn't a tapping your foot or drumming your pencil on the table kind of anxiousness. It's an excited but confident kind of waiting—hope filled, looking to the horizon, knowing something is going to happen and expecting to see God at work.

When we're confident that God has our best in mind, we can be patient and give Him all the room He needs to work on our behalf. We can fully rest, focusing on His goodness rather than our need. The waiting no longer distracts, but rather propels us to the feet of the One who will make all things right again in the end.

Like a comforted child, we can be confident moms—confident of God's provision and His protection, content to simply be wherever God has placed us.

All the Good Things

Not Yets and Daydreams

To Remember

- It's up to us how we'll care for what we've already been given.
- Our healthy desires are *good*. Our being in a funk about the timing of them is not.
- We can be confident moms—confident of God's provision and His protection, content to simply be wherever God has placed us.

To Hold On To

Finally, brothers, whatever is true, whatever is honorable, whatever is just, whatever is pure, whatever is lovely, whatever is commendable, if there is any excellence, if there is anything worthy of praise, think about these things (Philippians 4:8).

Wait for the LORD; be strong, and let your heart take courage; wait for the LORD! (Psalm 27:14).

Let the words of my mouth and the meditation of my heart be acceptable in your sight, O LORD, my rock and my redeemer (Psalm 19:14).

To Consider

Our daydreams have the potential to lead us into some unhealthy thought patterns. Write a few words, turning one of your daydreams into a prayer to the Lord.

_____

_____

_____

Part Six

When Life Takes a Turn

21

Looking Up Long Enough to See

Amanda

May the God of hope fill you with all joy and peace in believing, so that by the power of the Holy Spirit you may abound in hope.

ROMANS 15:13

In the books of Matthew, Mark, and Luke in the Bible, a story is told about a woman who had been bleeding abnormally for 12 years straight. Maybe she had uterine fibroids, obstetric fistula after becoming a young mom, or some other reproductive complication. We don't know. But the text says she spent all she had on doctors and nothing worked.

Then she reached out to touch the edge of Jesus's garment.

I feel like this would be the right place to insert a few sparkly star emojis or praise hands. This woman was deemed culturally unclean and was ostracized for carrying a burden she was forced to bear—one she never asked for. That was the life she was given. This was probably the trial that kept her humble, dependent, and searching for a better way. *Surely this isn't all there is for me,* she must have thought.

And then Jesus walked by.

Mark 5:27-28 says, "She had heard the reports about Jesus and came up behind him in the crowd and touched his garment. For she said, 'If I touch even his garments, I will be made well.'"

Her desire became a reality, because as she touched His outer garment, she was instantly healed. I wonder if she sat at home planning it out in her head beforehand, like I would have: *If I ever see Jesus out and about, I'm going to touch His clothing. Yes, I am. Even if He doesn't acknowledge me, even if I'm scared, because He's my answer.*

Isn't this sort of like what we do when we think about the possibility of meeting someone important to us? *What would I say? What would they do? Would I freeze? Would they think I'm ridiculous? Could this even happen?*

Or what if she impulsively reached out to Jesus in faith as He moved through the crowd with only a hefty dose of adrenaline to accompany her boldness? In that time, a woman touching a man in public was socially unacceptable. And we must remember she was deemed unclean because of her condition and would have been shunned by everyone who knew her. *Sadness.*

I get a tingle in my chest when I imagine being the woman in this scene. I mean, can you even picture it? Jesus is there in person, and He walks right by you. Your need for Him is greater than you could ever say, and the time is now. You aren't *supposed* to touch His garment, but you reach out and touch it anyway.

How she must have suffered those years leading up to this moment. It's easy for us to read this tiny little passage in our great big Bibles and not even think about the unwritten backstory, a part of the story hidden as it is with all of us. This woman had a past that grieved her, one we have very little insight into, but what God wants us to see most of all is that she was healed by the King of kings, who was standing right there in the flesh. Just like that.

What I love about this woman, although her story is brief in all three biblical tellings, is that *she* approached Jesus. She didn't hang back and wish He would notice her among all the others pressing against Him that day. She had faith that if she could simply get close to Him, something could happen. So *she* moved toward *Him*.

I wrote earlier about the ongoing physical pain in my body that's the result of a car accident in my teens and that forced me to quit exercising. I've suffered much over the years. I've paid doctors thousands and thousands of dollars to find relief and prayed just as many prayers. I've missed countless events and opportunities, and tears and heartbreak have taken over at several points. But I've also spent as much time on faith and hope.

I imagine the woman with this bleeding problem went through all these stages as well. Suffering. Doctors. Prayer. Missing out. Heartbreak. Faith. Hope. Possibly over and over, only to come up wanting. *Again.*

Maybe the day she touched Jesus was the first day she decided to hope and put her faith in Him. We don't know, but what matters is that she got there.

My mind naturally wanders into what-if mode in situations like this. What if she'd been so distracted by the pain and sadness that she never went to see Jesus that day? What if she had stayed depressed and kept herself holed up? What if she had never come to the place of hope? She had every earthly reason not to have hope, but she knew that although nothing earthly could help her, there was an unearthly presence about Jesus. He was as unordinary as they came, and she placed all her unmet hopes on Him.

We all know what it feels like to let hope fade in and out of our lives. Our kids can tell when we've faded. Our smile disappears and we're a walking billboard for the saddest thing you ever saw. It feels like nothing will change, and we think we're stuck in this present, horrible reality forever. We keep our heads down—working, helping, fixing, hurting, and enduring.

I was in this place last week. It was Thanksgiving of all times, and

I didn't know how I was going to go on. The muscles in my neck and back were locked up and the headaches were unbearable. I was bone weary of the stress in my family life too. It all came crashing down, and I was forced to put a halt to everything. My bed was the only place I wanted to be, though it felt like a prison. I didn't want to lie down. I didn't want to feel so bad. I just wanted to live my normal life without the pain and stress.

But that wasn't my real life. My real life was present with me in that bed. My real life was sad and painful at that moment. I was in a dark place, so fed up with this cycle of pain in my body and weariness as a wife and mom. The easiest thing for me to do was give up.

But easy has never been the way to promise. Easy has never been the way to accomplish anything worthwhile. It wasn't easy for Jesus to give His life for ours. *Certainly not.*

Easy has never been the way to accomplish anything worthwhile.

When we're in that dark and scary place, where we aren't sure if we'll ever see the light of a happy day again, we have to look up. We must fight for hope. The woman in our story certainly did. She got up, took her eyes off her own sorrow, and looked for Jesus.

Jesus isn't walking in the flesh down our own dusty streets where we can see Him, but He is here. It makes me exceedingly excited to know I'll see Him face-to-face one day, but I also need to be mindful that He's here with me now. He's not only living within me, but the Holy Spirit is residing in every believer—the one beside me at church, the one in the next lane of traffic, and the one at my dinner table each night.

The woman who touched His garment didn't have the benefit of the Holy Spirit living inside her. We do. She didn't have the advantage of having the whole of Scripture to hold in her hands to ingest daily. We do. She was the recipient of unbelievable healing, but so are we. Will we keep trusting God even if our healing comes in a different way? In a different package? At a different time?

In Lysa TerKeurst's book *The Best Yes*, she reminds us that, as we're in the middle of making decisions, "We will steer where we stare."[1] Whatever we're focusing on will be the direction we'll eventually go. If we're down about our life and pain, we'll be down. If we're frustrated about our kids' lack of progress, we'll be frustrated. We don't realize how often we let our thoughts dictate our feelings and actions.

I don't want to be a woman who stays fixated on what's wrong. I want to be a woman who looks up long enough to see the God who will "fill you with all joy and peace in believing, so that by the power of the Holy Spirit you may abound in hope" (Romans 15:13).

22

Your Devastation Is Not a Distraction

Amanda

Safety does not rest in our distance from the danger, but in our nearness to God.

ANONYMOUS

Seven-year-old Levi jumped into the van in the school pick-up line, holding a special bag. When he showed me the award inside, I was crushed.

The ceremony Jeremy and I had been invited to attend had been on the calendar for weeks. We'd even signed and returned a notice promising we'd attend. Levi had been struggling at school because of some special needs, and we were just so crazy proud his teacher had chosen him out of his whole first grade class to be honored with an award among the other *Terrific Kids* in his school.

But we'd missed it. We'd planned for it, were thrilled about it, yet still somehow missed it. He was all alone in the cafeteria that morning with no family to cheer him on like we'd promised we would be. The school sent a staff member to be by his side in our place.

Insert a big, fat dagger to my heart.

Tears ran hot from behind my sunglasses and down my face and neck in the van that day, and I had to turn down the depressing-ish song on the radio as we turned out of the school parking lot. I just couldn't believe it. *How could we? Why were we so forgetful?*

But wait. Of *course* we missed it.

It might seem a little much to be moved to tears about missing a school celebration that my squirrelly son would probably forget all about by the next day, but what lay beneath a simple story of forgetfulness and regret was the story that revealed something more. A great devastation had hit our family just ten days prior, and missing this event was one more sad thing to add to the pile of wreckage affecting us.

I hadn't slept in days. I didn't have an appetite. That Wednesday was the first day I hadn't cried in ten straight days—that is, until I realized what we'd missed. But I wasn't as upset about not remembering this event as I was about the pain that had stolen our regular lives.

Hard times and consuming adversity are thieves. They steal our ability to think, our capacity to see very far or clearly, and our energy and strength. Devastation steals, and it must be dealt with, but it's not a distraction. It's a reality.

Your devastation is not a distraction.

Working through wreckage isn't a diversion from focusing on the most important things; it becomes the most important thing. At times we fixate wrongly on our disappointments, and that can be considered a distraction, for sure. But taking care of ourselves and dealing with devastating situations in a healthy way? No, ma'am. We need to do that. I've lived long enough to experience plenty of my own deep devastation and spoken to enough women to know that pain cannot be ignored. Nor are we wronging our families and people who depend on us by attending to it.

The pain you're experiencing is not a deviation from your real life, though sometimes we get mad at adversity because it seems to interrupt our real life. Hear me say this: Your pain *is* your real life right now. We hate to hear that. We hate to live that. But it's real, and we've got to stop living in guilt because we think we're doing a disservice to ourselves, our families, and others when we're working through pain.

We *must* work through it. We must live our lives despite it and with it and do everything our regular life requires of us too. Pain is horrible. Pain is unwelcome. But getting help and getting healthy is neither of those things.

> **Pain is horrible. Pain is unwelcome. But getting help and getting healthy is neither of those things.**

As we've all experienced, we inflict some forms of pain on ourselves, and then some forms of pain are inflicted on us by others, and still other forms of pain reach us for reasons we may never know in this life.

When we're grieving or at a loss and don't want to push away the pain but deal with it in an honest and God-honoring way, a sure and steady place to turn is the Psalms. In the Psalms, as you'll notice when you read through them, a shift takes place in passages that speak of hardship and grief.

At the start, the pain is evident and slowly addressed, though not erased. Then in the end the author has worked his way back to God.

Psalm 69 is an example. David begins speaking about his current situation in verses 1 through 4:

> Save me, O God!
>   For the waters have come up to my neck.
> I sink in deep mire,
>   where there is no foothold;
> I have come into deep waters,
>   and the flood sweeps over me.
> I am weary with my crying out;
>   my throat is parched.

My eyes grow dim
     with waiting for my God.

More in number than the hairs of my head
     are those who hate me without cause;
mighty are those who would destroy me,
     those who attack me with lies.
What I did not steal
     must I now restore?

David tells of his troubles—the hurt and the hopelessness that tie his mind up in knots. Then further down, starting in verse 13 and on through 18, he asks God for help:

But as for me, my prayer is to you, O LORD.
     At an acceptable time, O God,
          in the abundance of your steadfast love answer me in
               your saving faithfulness.
Deliver me
     from sinking in the mire;
let me be delivered from my enemies
     and from the deep waters.
Let not the flood sweep over me,
     or the deep swallow me up,
     or the pit close its mouth over me.

Answer me, O LORD, for your steadfast love is good;
     according to your abundant mercy, turn to me.
Hide not your face from your servant,
     for I am in distress; make haste to answer me.
Draw near to my soul, redeem me;
     ransom me because of my enemies!

David processes his emotions and harsh feelings in prayer toward those who've wronged him in the next section, and then he honors God and gets his mind in the right place. Verses 30 to 36 end the psalm with these heartfelt words:

I will praise the name of God with a song;
    I will magnify him with thanksgiving.
This will please the Lord more than an ox
    or a bull with horns and hoofs.
When the humble see it they will be glad;
    you who seek God, let your hearts revive.
For the Lord hears the needy
    and does not despise his own people who are prisoners.

Let heaven and earth praise him,
    the seas and everything that moves in them.
For God will save Zion
    and build up the cities of Judah,
and people shall dwell there and possess it;
    the offspring of his servants shall inherit it,
    and those who love his name shall dwell in it.

Looking to God's Word and following its pattern in our devastating times won't make our pain go away, but it can help us deal with our unhealthy feelings about them. When we're lower than we ever thought possible, may we let our children and others see how we rise, gripping the hand of the Rock of Ages as He pulls us out of the mess and holds us close.

23

Living in a Pain-Shaped Reality

Anne-Renee

Pain is…a good clarifier and a great teacher.
Nichole Nordeman[1]

have had a painful, pulsating headache for a little more than two and a half weeks now, a constant squeezing of pressure from my forehead to the base of my neck. It's a reminder that I'm a mere mortal made from dust and bone and rapidly returning to such a humble state.

Sadly, this continuous throbbing has been affecting my daily duties. Pain makes me cranky. It's been disturbing my work routine and regular ministry responsibilities, as well as my ability to drive to-and-fro and from here to there, which pretty much sums up all my taxi mom obligations during these busy middle school and high school years. It's been influencing my usual, mostly patient parental reactions to silliness, disobedience, eye rolling, homework squabbling, and teenage sarcasm. Not to mention my capacity to write, podcast, think clearly, and speak in complete sentences.

You see, every once in a while my body likes to remind me that I'm a woman living with the reality of a body twisted by scoliosis. Similar to Amanda, pain has become an intimate companion, playing a major role in my everyday life and struggle for perspective. And although I do my best to keep up with exercises, vitamins, and therapeutic techniques, I cannot seem to escape the natural way my bones like to curl and curve. I know this won't always be the case, and that someday my body will be made whole again through the beautiful reality of a new heaven and a new earth.

However, this knowledge does little to lessen the frustration of hurting in the moment. So I look to others for proper perspective, those who struggle with real life-altering, joy-sucking pain. Folks who have lost so much more than I have—jobs, homes, limbs, family members, spouses, health, marriages.

Suddenly my aching back and pounding head don't seem quite so important, so all-consuming. This excruciating signal of pain is a sign of life. A good life. A full life.

The pain is also a cautionary road sign prompting me to slow down and take stock of what's truly important, reminding me of my need for a Helper, a Rescuer, and a Redeemer. How each breath, although filled with pulsing pain, is a gift. A granting of grace I don't deserve.

And so I breathe in His goodness, and I exhale praise. For in the good, in the hard, and in the difficult, He is still God. His righteousness and unconditional love for us are not dependent upon our feeling A-OK or for everything to be right with the world. Our situations may be far from peaceful, full of hurt and falling apart, and yet the Prince of Peace still reigns. Still loves. Still desires to be in relationship with us, drawing us to Himself, desiring our hearts to fully trust in His sovereignty.

Our situations may be far from peaceful, yet the Prince of Peace still reigns.

He alone is our refuge. Our stronghold. Our ever-present help. The Rock on which we can lean and depend. Psalm 61:1-2 says, "Hear my cry, O God, listen to my prayer; from the end of the earth I call to you when my heart is faint. Lead me to the rock that is higher than

I." Sometimes I think He allows hardships so that in the comparative contrast of suffering, His glory may have the limelight.

Yes, life's storms can still be ugly and overwhelm us; they may even drown us for a season. But the growth that comes from those storms also has the potential of bringing overwhelming beauty.

Here's how the apostle Paul regarded this concept:

> To keep me from becoming conceited…a thorn was given me in the flesh, a messenger of Satan to harass me, to keep me from becoming conceited. Three times I pleaded with the Lord about this, that it should leave me. But he said to me, "My grace is sufficient for you, for my power is made perfect in weakness." Therefore I will boast all the more gladly of my weaknesses, so that the power of Christ may rest upon me. For the sake of Christ, then, I am content with weaknesses, insults, hardships, persecutions, and calamities. For when I am weak, then I am strong (2 Corinthians 12:7-10).

I love how His power is perfected through our weaknesses. Seriously—only God could turn something the world would define as calamity into something victorious. As C.S. Lewis wrote, "We can ignore even pleasure. But pain insists upon being attended to. God whispers to us in our pleasures, speaks in our conscience, but shouts in our pains: it is his megaphone to rouse a deaf world."[2]

Pain can also be an effective signal to others of our need for help, a beautiful flare of beckoning giving warmth to friendship and enlarging and expanding our hearts for one another.

Unfortunately, I have not handled my "thorn in the flesh" very well through the years. I tend to hide away when dealing with insurmountable bouts of discomfort, refusing to ask for help and holing up in the darkened shadows of my home. I like to disappear when pain arrives with all its bulky, bothersome luggage on my doorstep. Like an awkward teen with a glaring zit, I feel self-conscious and embarrassed.

But blanketing ourselves with misery and self-pity is not the gasoline God intended for us to fuel our relationships, and yet so often we allow pain to have the last word. We give it direct access to guide our emotions and dictate our actions, while giving ourselves a pass on living because of our current state.

As a result, we step back—from parenting, loving, serving, extending, growing, and discipling. We open wide the doors, offering pain an exclusive member pass to our day and our calendar, putting all other areas of life on hold because of this all-encompassing distraction.

The pain, whether physical or emotional, creates an obstacle, hiding us from the outside world, keeping us from pursuing our relationship with God, and constructing an all-consuming blockade of ache and anguish.

The issue is not the pain itself, but the barrier it creates that keeps us from pursuing what matters most: our faith, our families—and the calling to "go therefore":

"Go therefore and make disciples of all nations" (Matthew 28:19).

Thankfully, pain won't have the final word. The last word belongs to the One who is the Beginning and the End. The One who holds the world in the palm of His hand. The Author of all and the Sustainer of all. And it is in Him that we live and breathe—pain free or not.

24

You Don't Hear Me Saying *Yes, Please* to Stress

Anne-Renee

Every night I try to get eight hours of sleep in four hours.

Anonymous

It was Christmas Day. And instead of celebrating the Savior, instead of savoring the glorious time of year we set aside to remember and rejoice in the miraculous Gift, I was sitting in my car, in my garage, crying my exhausted little eyeballs out.

I had bitten off more than I could chew, having filled my head with images of the picture-perfect holiday, and I was now feeling overwhelmed by the stress of it all—too many meals requiring my supervision, too many extra mouths to feed in my home, too much Christmas. I was done—like, put a fork in me done.

Regrettably, I was way beyond receiving gracious pep talks from my well-meaning family, and way past all rational thought or action. What should have been a joyous day now left me feeling fried and jaded. I couldn't function. Couldn't celebrate. Couldn't breathe.

So there I sat, tears streaming and heart aching.

I knew this was my own fault. I had set up these crazy pie-in-the-sky expectations for myself, and when those expectations didn't come to fruition, my dreams of the ideal Christmas shattered into a million pieces. Fluttering shards of disappointment and feelings of failure rained down through the salty tears. What an epic failure! I was a total flop as a host. I began to wonder if I could maybe hide out in my car until the new year.

Somehow Christmas had become a reflection of me and how well I could pull off an impressive holiday, rather than a day set aside to celebrate Emmanuel, God with Us. Instead of Christmas carols and a reading of Luke 2, my stress and numerous to-dos had ruled and defined the day. Unlike something unavoidable, like severe weather or an unexpected trip to the ER, this dilemma was clearly self-induced, chosen by me and fully implemented by me.

My forgetfulness in what the day was all about was merely an indication of what was going on inside of me—exposing my hidden desire for appreciation and accolades. Instead of urging my guests to honor the true guest of honor, Jesus, I had endeavored to pocket all that praise and glory for myself.

Upon this heartbreaking realization, my tears doubled. "I'm sorry, Lord," I whispered into the quietness of the car. And to my surprise, the stillness spoke back: *My daughter, I'm here.*

In hindsight, it seems trivial to have gotten so worked up over a Christmas meal. But I bet if we were to go around the table and tell about a past memorable birthday or holiday, you might have a similar anecdote to share. And wouldn't you know it, we're not the only ones.

In Luke 12:22-34, Jesus had to have a little chat with His disciples about stressing out over the unimportant. His first examples of what not to worry about were food and clothing. (And all the mothers, especially those who struggle with weekly grocery shopping, not to mention school supply lists and back-to-school clothes, said *amen*.)

How many times have I as a mom stressed out over what to make for dinner...or getting through the never-ending piles of laundry? My first world problems come out in the form of not *if* we will get to eat, but *what* we'll get to eat—how to produce something magical with the paltry routine items in my pantry and freezer. And not *if* we have money to buy clothes, but how in the world we'll get them all clean and back into their drawers and closet homes.

We stress over the superficial and lose sight of the significant. We focus long and hard on the temporary, forgetting it's fleeting. Short-term. Passing. Momentary. Literally only here for a moment.

Stressing over the superficial causes us to lose sight of the significant.

We know in our heads that if God can take care of the birds of the air, He can (and will) take care of us. Goodness, He's incredible, amazing at clothing grass and arraying lilies. But when it comes down to it, we put ourselves back into the driver's seat, forgetting the One who is all—and *over* all. We rush around like chickens with our heads cut off, attempting to polish and preen our lives and our homes so others will be impressed. Wooing more but listening less. Working hard but losing the moment.

At the end of the day, we may be victorious on our own little battlefields, but at the same time be losing the long-term, big-picture war with perspective. We forget that life, in its worth and value, is way more important than food and much more significant than clothing (Luke 12:23). Consequently, our faith remains small, our point of view slim, and our stress too overwhelming. As Ann Voskamp describes in her book *One Thousand Gifts*, "Stress can be an addiction and worry can be our lunge for control and we forget the answer to this moment is always yes because of Christ."[1]

Like our worrywart friends, the disciples, we often choose to stress over the unknown details of what-might-be rather than rest in the reality of God's glorious what-will-be. Who are we to question His methods or quiz Him over His timing? Luke 12:32 reminds us, "Fear not, little flock, for it is your Father's good pleasure to give you the kingdom."

Allowing stress, whether self-induced or uninvited, to rule my heart and mind blinds me from seeing His hand and cripples my ability to see His fingerprints on the one life He has given me. Hands down, His purposes and plans trump anything I could ever formulate or attempt to execute.

If I'm serious about pursuing this undistracted life, I need to learn to say goodbye to self-induced pressure and hello to resting in what He may have for me, regardless of what it is. Because I know He has my best in mind. All day. Every day.

All the Good Things

When Life Takes a Turn

To Remember

- Your devastation is not a distraction.
- Pain is horrible. Pain is unwelcome. But getting help and getting healthy is neither of those things.
- Our situations may be far from peaceful, yet the Prince of Peace still reigns.
- Stressing over the superficial causes us to lose sight of the significant.

To Hold On To

Hear my cry, O God, listen to my prayer; from the end of the earth I call to you when my heart is faint. Lead me to the rock that is higher than I (Psalm 61:1-2).

May the God of hope fill you with all joy and peace in believing, so that by the power of the Holy Spirit you may abound in hope (Romans 15:13).

To Consider

Think of a time of pain, devastation, or self-induced stress.

- How did God reveal Himself to you during that time?
- What did you take away from that season or moment?

Part Seven

The Daily Derailing

25

Brain Held Hostage

Amanda

*I used to have functioning brain cells, but
I traded them in for children.*

ANONYMOUS

The brain's limbic system is responsible for memory. These last few years, however, my limbic system must have decided to ditch remembering things for me in favor of a pool party of sorts, where my brain cells swim around and play Marco Polo all day long.

It's been a steep decline, and I just don't get it.

What I do get is that I have lots of children. They ask lots of questions. They talk a lot. They need a lot. They are so very loud. Maybe my brain is on strike or overheated, or it's zoning out, scrolling through the bestsellers on Amazon while I fumble to figure stuff out on my own.

Speaking of asking questions…One day, after a particularly exasperating week as a mom, I decided to count the questions my kids asked me in a day. At the time, I think I had six, maybe seven kids, and one of them was probably a baby and not of question-asking age.

I leaned over the kitchen island with a pen and paper nearby and started working on my laptop. I looked at the clock: 9:07 a.m. *Ready, go. Let's see how many questions my children ask me today.*

Click-clack went my fingers on the laptop, and in no time flat, the first question came at me. Calmly, I answered it and left one careful tally mark on my paper. The asking escalated quickly, and before I could do anything worthwhile on my computer, it was 9:37 a.m., and I had answered 30 questions. In 30 minutes. *Thirty questions.*

I gave up and went to hyperventilate in my bedroom for a few minutes before showing my face again, and then I concluded that *life is just like this right now.*

Even though I don't have babies or preschoolers anymore, I still have eight children, and the questions are nonstop. All day. Every day. It sounds strange, but I'm sure you understand: It's so hard to function and focus when you're peppered with the need to stop and think when you're trying to...

- have a coherent thought for yourself
- read a recipe, email, text, book, or article
- use the restroom without visitors
- talk on the phone
- sleep
- pray or read the Bible
- stare out the window
- drive in peace
- write
- have a conversation

Did I mention sleep?

Even when I put on a movie, they still ask me questions:

Can I have a snack? *No, not right now.*

Can I sit with you for a minute? This part of the movie makes me sad. *Yes, please.*

Was the first telephone in use before or after the World Wars? *Um, we'll have to look that up.*

Mom, do you know you've got a text? *Thank you, but I set my phone across the room on purpose.*

Then there's breaking up fights, asking them to stop jumping around and sit back down when the movie gets "boring," and saying to them, *Please don't sit so close to the TV screen.*

Interruptions aren't always bad. Kids are kids, and they need us. Moms have an important job to do, and our children need and desire our attention. But we're also people with other responsibilities, too, and we have brains that need some room to think and then decide to take some actions.

If you're plagued with daily headaches or other chronic pain like me, thinking and focusing are even more difficult. *Jesus, help.*

We'd like our brains to function well. We'd love to be attentive mothers, ready to look our kids in the eye and truly love them. But how do we do that when our brains are held hostage by so many thoughts, to-dos, and questions coming at us?

I don't know if this will help you, but my husband and I have had to set some pretty hefty boundaries to keep our kids from running all over us. We've got nearly every age and stage covered, as well as some special needs, and we'd go plum crazy if we let things get as out of control as they naturally could.

One of the boundaries has to do with how the kids communicate with me.

First, we moms seem to receive all the questions, don't we? Even if Dad's in the room with them, the children roam the house searching for me—sometimes because I'm the one who might give them a yes. (Even my teens do this.) We're working on this tendency.

We also needed a solution to combat their tendency to assume

I can pick words meant for me out of the air when all ten of our voices are speaking at the same time (which happens at all hours of the day, except the sleeping hours) or when I'm already occupied. Our kids are taught to say, "Excuse me, Mom," when it appears to be a decent time to ask me something. If I look them in the eye and say, "Yes, [insert name]?" then it's time to talk to me or ask one of those questions.

But if they just start talking, I don't answer even if I heard them. It's hard not to answer them anyway, but that wouldn't teach them a thing except that Mom will answer no matter what, so there's no need to be polite.

This might sound harsh or rude, but I can't stand at attention all the time, waiting for someone to talk to me. I might as well set up a booth like Lucy in the Peanuts gang does and sit there all day, open for business. This boundary is as much for my sanity as it is to teach our kids good manners and that every thought that pops into their heads doesn't need to be voiced to Mom, or even said out loud in the first place.

Does this boundary work perfectly? No. A child will still start talking to me while I'm occupied, such as in a conversation or when I'm writing. I hear them, but I'll not answer them. They'll stare at me, baffled, wondering why in the world I'm not answering. After a bit of time passes, I ask them why they thought I didn't answer. Every time they say, "Ohhhh! I didn't say 'Excuse me, Mom.'"

Our older children are much better with this. Our younger three, at ages six to eight, still aren't the very best at it, but it takes time to see a difference after setting a boundary with kids.

It takes time to see a difference after setting a boundary with kids.

Yes, it's exhausting to keep reminding them about this, but in the long run it's worth the time we take to teach this skill. It helps them with their family and peer relationships, at church, at school, and when speaking to people in general.

Our mom brains need white space, and maybe, just maybe, a little bit of that space can be had after all.

I pray your frazzly mind finds some space to think, create, and feel like a person. But until then, don't count how many questions you're asked in a day. *Just don't.*

26

Saying Welcome with Your Life

Amanda

I'm convinced generous people are the happiest.

Kristen Welch[1]

When I was a kid, I felt the most welcome in my parents' lives when they listened to me, looked up from what they were doing to notice me, and showed up at school events to cheer me on. It felt like my life mattered to them and that I was a happy addition to theirs. I never felt neglected or left behind while they pursued their goals. We kids weren't seen as appendages creating roadblocks to their best lives.

Through the years my mom sewed dresses for the two of us girls for major holidays and school dances. I remember thinking it was fun to stay up late for final fitting sessions by the glow of the sewing machine light the night before an event. I felt like I was special to my mom. She was willing to spend time on me and for me.

Another time I knew my mom cherished me was when she'd take me to the local bookstore at the mall when there was a new release in my favorite series. High five to my fellow Sweet Valley Twins fans who geeked out over Elizabeth and Jessica Wakefield as much as I did.

Whenever we went to Waldenbooks, I'd spend $3.75 on a new paperback and have it read before we got home from running errands. My mom would laugh in astonishment every time. I could feel the joy I brought her. It will always stick with me. She made me feel like my passions and I were important to her.

My dad was known throughout our high school because he showed up for the dances my sister and I attended. He got out on the floor to groove to the music with us at the urging of our friends. I'm not kidding. He even showed up at the prom to lean over the balcony and see how we were all getting along. He was fun, and we reveled in the fact that everyone knew and loved him too. That made *us* feel loved. It might have mortified the heck out of many of you, but to us it was the greatest.

In high school, my sister and I had a beloved classmate with special needs, and she would call the house every week or so just to talk to "Dad." We'd get a chance to chat with her for a quick minute, but we knew the real reason she liked to call. Dad would take the phone with a twinkle in his eye and talk with her like they were old pals—teasing her in all the ways that were guaranteed to make her roar with laughter. We could hear her through the receiver, and sometimes she'd laugh until she could barely breathe. When we saw her at school the next day, we were sure to hear all about it—what Dad had said and how funny she thought he was.

He delighted in what we delighted in, and that made us feel incredibly welcome in his world.

Maybe it comes down to this: I don't remember having to vie for either of my parents' attention. They might remember it differently, but I don't recall begging or waiting for them to look up from what they were doing or away from the TV to notice me.

But I see my kids needing to do that with me—too often. *Gulp.*

Granted, I have more kids than my parents did, and they could focus on their full-time work outside the home while their children were at school or daycare, so I don't want to romanticize them or say they were less distracted than I am as a parent. But I do know they seemed to make the most of the time they had with me.

You might be reading this wishing your own parents were as attentive. Perhaps the way your parents were with you has cast a long shadow over you and how you mother your children—especially if wounds of abuse have stacked up. I know all too many people who share your story, and I want to say I'm sorry.

Billy Graham said parenting is as simple as showing love. "Love your children," he said, "and let them know you love them. Children who experience love find it far easier to believe God loves them."[2]

When we pay attention to our children, we're showing love—therefore displaying God's love for them through us. It really is that simple. My life says *Welcome!* to my kids when I show them God's beautiful welcome of them through Jesus, yet we make it so, so complicated.

We love our kids by showing them how God feels about them:

He is constantly aware of them.

He is ever-forgiving of them.

He never forgets about them.

His love for them is unwavering.

We love our kids by showing them how God feels about them.

These ways to love are tricky. I'm not constantly aware of my kids, I'm not always very forgiving, and I've had the startling realization that too many times I can even become forgetful when it comes to my kids. And let's not talk about all the ways I've loved them conditionally through the years.

We can't be exactly like God, but we can do *something*. We can emulate Him as best we know how. That could look like...

- looking them in the eye
- setting boundaries for our distractions
- paying attention when they speak
- using kind words and a kind tone of voice
- sharing the gospel with them often
- reminding them of their worth
- forgiving them quickly
- patiently responding to their questions (Ooh. Remember the last chapter?)
- spending focused moments with them each day
- smiling when they catch your eye
- remembering to show them affection

This feels a little more doable, doesn't it? Perfection isn't necessary, but persistence certainly is.

Perfection isn't necessary, but persistence certainly is.

When we invite guests over for dinner or for a playdate, our responsibility to them doesn't end at the door after we've taken their coats. For them to feel accepted in our presence and our home, we need to pour into them over and over throughout their stay. Our actions should say *Welcome!* right along with our homes.

We greet guests by looking them in the eye, offering them something to drink, showing them where the bathroom is, asking them questions, and eventually sitting down to talk, all while remaining focused on them. It isn't enough to invite people into our homes and then allow them to waste away in the entryway—no. There's more to be done and said.

You could say the same for our children. It isn't enough that they were born; we need to help them grow in all the ways kids need to grow. The act of welcoming our kids is repeated in many ways for the duration of their growing-up time. We feed them, we clothe them, we take care of all their needs, sure, but if we don't invite them into our sphere with our faces, our tone and volume, our actions, our time, and the words we say, what do we accomplish?

We aren't robots; we don't have endless pools of time and energy to dip from when we need it. So how we spend the time and energies we *do* have is important.

Are these beloved humans most accustomed to being greeted by our foreheads and the tops of our heads when they come into a room or as they silently (or rather loudly) wish we'd look their direction? We peer down at our phones, computers, recipes, books, projects, and work so readily, but are we paying attention to our children as closely as we do to all those things? Paying attention to their faces? To their lives?

I'm convicted every time I fail at this. It's impossible for me to miss the twinge of the Holy Spirit as He gently prods me to go a different way. I know I'm in the wrong when I insist on keeping my preferred time line for what I want to be doing in the moment. Sometimes the kids need to wait while I finish a task, but sometimes I need to make myself wait. The difference is discernment.

I admit, though, that sometimes I ignore the Spirit's tap-tap-tap on my shoulder. It's like that tiny angel and the bright red devil on Kronk's shoulders in the movie *The Emperor's New Groove*, as if they're standing there, duking it out, exchanging choice words while I decide what I'm going to do. Will I stay stuck in do-not-disturb mode and tune out my kids? Or will I set aside what I'm doing in favor of focusing on my priority people?

27

That Dirty Word—Self-Control

Anne-Renee

*You will never look back on life and think, "I spent
too much time with my kids."*

Anonymous

When my children were small, we spent a great deal of time talking about sharing and making wise choices. This was back in the days of sippy cups, Gerber Puffs, and hearing lots of "Uh-oh. I sorry, Mama."

What usually followed such a sheepish, chubby-cheeked apology was a cleanup or phone call to Poison Control. Sometimes both.

Those years were filled to overflowing with numerous occasions to coach my little people. Instructing. Demonstrating. Explaining, "This is why we do this."

We had lotion mishaps. Hair gel art shows. Curious attempts at fixing squeaks in rocking chairs—not with WD-40, mind you, but with Daddy's cologne. Washing the bathroom mirror with hand soap. Learning important life lessons, like how to take proper care of a watch, which means not bathing it in a glass of water and then trying to correct the problem by putting it in the clothes dryer.

All it took was two minutes of Mom using the bathroom or

starting a load of laundry, and suddenly we were knee-deep in yet another toddler fiasco. The days seemed short and yet painfully long, full of adventure and with plenty of clarifying and communication opportunities.

Then there was the day we learned Mango Body Butter smells good, but it is *not* to be eaten. (That time I did call Poison Control, only to have the man on the other end of the phone tell me to stop panicking, to just give my son lots of water and that his poop might smell sweet for several days. *Awesome!* I'm pretty sure he was trying his best to maintain composure while talking to me. His voice sounded all choke-y, like he was holding back a giant laugh. I can't really blame him, though. The whole scenario sounded bonkers, even to my ears.)

The hours were filled with constant reminders, gentle promptings, and times of teaching, making each mistake and misunderstanding into a way to learn. You know, the basics—like sharing, kindness, and self-control. Things like "This is why we don't hit or kick our siblings," "This is why we don't put gum in our hair," and "This is why we always try to use the bathroom before going anywhere in the car, especially on a long trip."

Although I did my best to eliminate that selfish word *mine* from my children's vocabulary, it snuck in anyway. They hid toys so they didn't have to share them. They hoarded favorite foods, pulling them to the side of their plates and covering them with their hands. And if forced to share? Oh the tears, wailing, sighing, huffing, and folding their arms as a sign of frustration and perceived injustice.

Those years with young children taught me a lot about my own sense of selfishness. The tendency to think my time was more important than my children's. The egocentric feeling that I'd earned a mom break—and the counting of minutes until said break. The nagging expectation of just wanting to get away for a bit. That internal ranting of, *"I deserve this!"*

Then there was the frustration of constantly being interrupted, questioned, and even corrected by my children. Oh how that rankled my senses.

As a mama running on little sleep, grabbing coffee and food only after making sure my kids were well taken care of and fed, a tiny seed of resentment began to take root. My needs, my wants, my demands—everything I felt was warranted as a hardworking mom—began to seep into my words and actions. Making sure my husband knew how hard I was laboring by dropping martyr hints and leaving piles of clean dishes and folded laundry out so he could see all I had accomplished throughout the day.

My mothering looked great from the outside, but inside was a whole different story.

Since nobody was going to award me my very own mommy break, I decided to take matters into my own hands. Morning was lie-in-bed-until-my-children-force-me-out-of-it Me Time. Devotional time and the kids' naptimes both turned into Me Time. A sense of idle entitlement crept in, along with some lovely companions: laziness and listlessness.

I wasn't exactly holed up in my bedroom eating bonbons, but I wasn't working on personal growth either. *Self-control* had become a dirty word. I didn't want to think about or embrace it, even though I knew it was the right thing to do and pursue. Quite thoroughly, I had convinced myself I didn't need rules or restraint in my personal life. I had earned that downtime and deserved a blessed break.

In that selfish season, I heard someone at a MOPS conference speak about intentional motherhood, about being deliberate and purposeful with our time. And that included our downtime, using each moment of our day to bring honor and glory to our Father in heaven. What a wake-up call that was! Here I'd been so focused on me and my deservedness, how I was justified in having a break, that I'd completely lost sight of living life for my God and my King. My eyes had been so fixated on my own doings, on how hard I was working and the hours I was cleaning and washing and fixing and teaching, that I'd lost sight of everything He had done and was continuing to do in my family and my life.

Self-control became something to pursue and practice again, controlling my distracting thought patterns and keeping those lazy tendencies in check.

I started sifting through my motives and my words, even in how I conversed with other moms. I asked God to keep a lid on my selfish tendencies and help me focus on serving Him and my family with a joyful heart, to help me chase what was best for my people versus what seemed best in the moment for me.

I'm not talking about martyrdom motherhood, but rather surrendered servanthood. There's a significant difference between the two. Martyrdom mothering is putting on a show, to encourage everyone around us to loudly applaud our efforts or to gain sympathy points for how much we're doing. A distracted heart sees value in what others see, but a giving heart sees value in what others do not see.

A distracted heart sees value in the seen.
A giving heart sees value in the unseen.

In stark contrast, surrendered servanthood is characterized by humility. Seeking the best of those we love, submitting our mind, will, and emotions to the One who created them in the first place.

I'm also not saying we shouldn't take breaks. Because goodness knows, we all need a break from time to time. We can serve our families so much better from a full tank than when we're running on empty. And hey, even Jesus understood the importance of taking a nap. (Can I get an amen?)

But if we say we want Him to be Lord over all, we must put into practice the act of giving Him our all, allowing Him Lordship in those hard places—in those aching, uncomfortable, difficult, and demanding areas we like to keep shrouded from the light of day, hidden in the shadows.

Scripture warns us that if we don't learn to have self-control, we will become slaves to what controls us: laziness, pursuit of wealth, gluttony, lust, greed. Whatever it is that's ruling our thoughts and actions. The only way to combat these controlling lies is with some hard-hitting truth. That's why spending time in the Bible is so important. Self-pity and selfishness have no foundation to stand on when compared to the truth of God's Word, for those words of life can transform and renew our minds, helping us make good choices and wise decisions, helping us in our mothering, in ministry, in marriage…in everything.

How we live becomes less about self-control and more about God control. Not a matter of how much we're losing, but the freedom we're gaining to love wholeheartedly, with no reservations or selfishness holding us back. It's an open-handed "Use me, God" approach to every day, trusting His guidance and keeping our ears attuned to the speaking and working of the Spirit. Thankfully, self-control is one of those fruits that comes from spending time with the Spirit, a natural outflowing from a life rooted in Him. We don't have to pursue it and earn it on our own.

But it won't be easy. Learning self-control requires us to give up our sense of entitlement, exchanging it for an attitude of discipleship. It means allowing the Spirit to lead us rather than being led by our own selfish propensities, parting ways with self-indulgence and ushering in a new life defined by self-control. That can mean only one thing: giving God complete control.

No more whining and cries of "mine" for this girl. The end.

28

When I Pile My Plate with Worry
Anne-Renee

*Today is mine. Tomorrow is none of my business. If I peer
anxiously into the fog of the future, I will strain my spiritual
eyes so that I will not see clearly what is required of me now.*

ELISABETH ELLIOT[1]

I looked out the window and watched the fluttering leaves dance through the air. Ugh. If only I could make them stay on the trees for one more week of glory.

We had company coming, and I really wanted them to see Alaska in its full autumn beauty. I wanted them to fall in love with the 49th state the way we had. But more importantly, I worried that if they didn't like what they saw, our dear friends wouldn't want to return for a second or third or fourth visit. I really missed the close fellowship we'd experienced with them before moving here.

I stared hard at the leaves still anchored on trees and willed them to stay there. Unfortunately, that didn't work, and the picturesque foliage dropped to the ground over the next few days.

I can't help but wonder how many times I've worried about what was clearly out of my control, the times I've agonized long and hard over laborious little details, irrelevant apprehensions, and unwarranted unnecessary concerns.

What if it's super windy and our event company's tents blow down? What if the bride hates our customer service and smears our company's reputation online?

What if the items in our store don't sell and we're stuck with all this inventory I just ordered? What if this downturn in the economy keeps going and we can't keep our doors open? What then? What will we do for work? How will we provide for our family?

These are the kinds of thoughts that run through your head when you own an event rental and party supply company—or at least they do for me.

And then there's regular life here in Alaska...

What if it snows? Will I be able to travel safely from point A to point B? What if school is canceled? What if my car slides into a ditch? What if my cell phone service is so poor there that I can't reach my husband to come and rescue me?

And those runaway fears...

What if one of our children gets hurt and I can't get to them quickly enough? What if I get hurt and can't take care of our family? What if I can't fulfill a ministry commitment? A work obligation? A specific deadline?

I remember worrying as a young mom about missing all the firsts—first words, first steps, first whatever it was. And here I am, an older, supposedly wiser woman, and still stressing about all sorts of things beyond my control:

- the kids' school schedules and grades, and what teachers they might have in the coming years (not to mention their friends, and their faith...)

- end-of-year sales reports at work (and we're only halfway through the year)

- travel plans and unreliable weather

- other people's reactions or opinions

- sickness (mine, my husband's, or the kids')

- the changing of seasons and changes in life
- who will my kids marry
- who will be our next president

The list is endless. These are the important and not-so-important concerns that keep me up at night. Not world hunger, world peace, or world-shaking earthquakes and tsunamis, but big what-ifs. Totally lame, I know.

As moms, we breathe worry as mindlessly as we breathe air. The thing is, though, we have nothing to show for our worry. Well, maybe a wrinkle or two and a few gray hairs, but worrying about a situation doesn't make it any better. Or as Jesus indicated in Matthew 6:27, it won't add a single hour to our lives. Worry just bogs us down and gets in the way of us living life fully.

So why do we do it? God didn't wire us to worry. He wired us to trust Him. Victor Hugo said, "Courage, then, and patience! Courage for the great sorrows of life, and patience for the small ones. And then when you have laboriously accomplished your daily task, go to sleep in peace. God is awake."[2]

God didn't wire us to worry. He wired us to trust.

I love how the hymn "Come, Thou Fount of Every Blessing" so eloquently puts it: "Prone to wander, Lord, I feel it. Prone to leave the God I love. Here's my heart, O take and seal it. Seal it for Thy courts above."[3]

We are inclined to wander. We're susceptible to deviating from the path God has set before us. So to fight these distracting worries and combat these useless fears, we must figure out how to push them aside.

Something I've started doing in the last few months is asking myself if I've done everything I can to be prepared in whatever the situation is that's bothering me. If I have, then the next step is one of laying it all down. That means stopping dead in my worrisome tracks, loosening my death grip of control, and giving that burden to the Lord. It's an act of letting go, of stepping back, trusting that He has it under control, and then following Him in obedience. It's all about releasing and resting. Of surrendering my anxieties, the what-ifs and what-could-bes. Holding nothing back, and giving Him my all.

Listing. Laying. Leaving.

Listing my worries.

Laying them down.

And…

Leaving them there.

List them out. Lay them down. Leave them there.

It sounds simple, but hard. Straightforward, but difficult. But trust me, it's a worthwhile wrestling and submission process that is foundational to freeing oneself from the fingers of worry that like to firmly wrap themselves around our mama hearts and minds.

In the convicting words of World War II survivor Corrie ten Boom, "If a care is too small to be turned into a prayer, it is too small to be made into a burden."[4]

What if instead of living in a state of anxiousness, we do a replacement of sorts and fill our minds with peace?

What if instead of living in a state of anxiousness, we do a replacement of sorts and fill our minds with peace? Real peace. Like asking for our daily bread in the Lord's Prayer. Asking for what we need today (and just for today) and not worrying about tomorrow.

Philippians 4:6-7 says, "Do not be anxious about anything, but in everything by prayer and supplication with thanksgiving let your requests be made known to God. And the peace of God, which surpasses all understanding, will guard your hearts and minds in Christ Jesus."

Right before these two action-packed verses Paul reminds us of something really mind-blowing. He says, "The Lord is at hand" (Philippians 4:5). Literally, the Lord is near. The fact that He is in close proximity suddenly gives a whole new perspective on the things that weigh us down. On our fears. On our worries. On all that junk interrupting our sleep and invading our rest. All the stuff that may or may not even happen. Let's be women pursuing peace rather than women who marinate our minds in fear. Let's do whatever it takes to keep our heads and hearts clear and open to the plan and purposes of our great God. Life's just too short to clog it all up with anxiety. It's too costly to shortchange it in exchange for a few worries and fears.

I propose a toast to searching and seeking out a worry-free plate, with a side of rest, accompanied by a satisfying breathing in of His peace. I sure don't need these worries, and I doubt you need them in your life either. It's hard enough to be a good mama without all this extra baggage hanging around. All it does is weigh us down, and no mother in the world needs more on her plate.

Well, unless it's a piece of chocolate cake. And then a teeny tiny slice might be just what she needs.

All the Good Things

The Daily Derailing

To Remember

- We love our kids by showing them how God feels about them.
- Perfection isn't necessary, but persistence certainly is.
- A distracted heart sees value in the seen. A giving heart sees value in the unseen.
- God didn't wire us to worry. He wired us to trust.

To Hold On To

Do not be anxious about anything, but in everything by prayer and supplication with thanksgiving let your requests be made known to God. And the peace of God, which surpasses all understanding, will guard your hearts and your minds in Christ Jesus (Philippians 4:6-7).

Let all that you do be done in love (1 Corinthians 16:14).

To Consider

- Decide what you'll set aside this week in favor of focusing on your priority people. Then do it.

Part Eight

Overcoming the Just Don't Wannas

29

When We Want It to
Be All Their Fault

Amanda

If you look for perfection, you'll never be content.

Leo Tolstoy[1]

I was so disappointed in myself. Why was I so irritable and eaten up inside? The living room floor was covered in a light layer of construction dust, piles of tools and *building* materials were lying around its edges, and overall it didn't look the way I preferred—sure. But really, why was this such a big deal?

Why couldn't I be okay no matter how my house looked on any given day? We *were* in the middle of a major remodel, for goodness' sake. But still, my thoughts immediately accused: *How weak am I? How swayed by my circumstances am I?*

How disappointing, both me and my house. One was a mess on the inside; the other was messy for all to see.

Of course, my poor house was simply doing what houses do. People live here—ten people, to be exact. We don't have a maid (dream world), so ten unpaid, non-employees are responsible for keeping up. Hmm. That explains *that*.

But what's wrong with *me*? Why am I so messy when I'm the only one who lives inside of me? I take a deep breath and let my exhale drag out as long as it can, because I know why: perfectionism.

My life and surroundings aren't meeting my standards, and it's left me defeated and disappointed. But my house and my very own self are not all that bother me; virtually everything does these days.

I've always been the easygoing wife, mom, and friend. The one who greets with a smile and a "no problem" attitude with my family and anyone I come across. It's a role I've played effortlessly for years on end, and I'm completely comfortable and happy playing it. It's who I am.

Then our family grew again, and I changed. Our new addition's personality was different from her siblings. Being a mom was no longer comfortable—well, as comfortable as mothering several kids can be. It felt like a circus before, and now it felt like war.

I loved my daughter with everything in me, yes. But it was just so hard. The older she got, the more I lost control. Nothing I could do as a mom changed the course she was careening down. We began to clash. I mean, really clash in her toddler and preschool years. And now as she continues to grow, it's the same, except she's taller and I'm older with a patch of gray around my temples.

She's got controlling tendencies, and I've pushed so hard against her desire for control that I've let myself become bitter and angry over how hard this is. Frankly, how hard I've perceived she's making this.

I'm a rule follower. She is not. Following rules is just an option to her. She believes forging her own path is often better, even if that means unpleasant consequences meet her over and over.

If I'm told to stop doing something, I want to stop. She pushes harder for her way, no matter how miserable it makes her life. I desire harmony and peace in my relationships. She's fine with angst and strain; they don't faze her in the least. She doesn't even realize this most of the time. She bides her time and consequences, and then she goes back to her old way. She seems to jump from trouble to trouble, whistling as she goes.

This is an ongoing struggle for mom and daughter, but the greatest good coming from mothering this child of mine has been how glaring it has made my own sin of perfectionism, pride, impatience, and anger—sin impossible to ignore.

Where did my easygoing personality go? All I know is that sin moved in and tucked the better version of me away for a time.

I don't think it's bad to desire harmony, peace, and general ease in your life and relationships, but I do think it's wrong to command it and cross the line of sin if you don't get it. My imperfection is no different than hers. Her sin is no better or worse than mine. She is responsible for hers, and I am responsible for mine.

She's also a child, and I am not.

My daughter, whom I love like crazy, isn't really the issue here. Our struggles show the process we all go through. We believe we struggle in certain areas of sin only because others push us to it. I've had those thoughts and expressed those words in several relationships.

I wouldn't struggle with perfectionism if these people weren't so messy. They force me to correct them.

I wouldn't have a tough time holding my tongue if everyone would speak kindly to me and with some common sense. Why can't we all just communicate well?

I wouldn't get angry if my kids would stop disregarding what I say and kindly do what I ask them to do. I'll never give them something that's too hard for them.

My hope for fun-loving interactions and happy family times is dashed over and over, and then I get bent out of shape, leaving a trail of harsh words and bitter sighs.

Life isn't what I thought it would be, that's for sure. But each day brings a new set of chances for me to react in a God-honoring way to the life and people I've been given. Will I continue to be distracted by my disappointment in myself, other people, and my circumstances and make it obvious to all? Or will I keep my mind in a good place with a faith that shows?

We know trials will come, yet how often are we surprised and embittered by them when they do?

In what is known as the Upper Room Discourse in the book of John, chapters 13–17, Jesus told His disciples they would inevitably face trials as they lived out the rest of their days on earth. All this was while they shared their last supper together before their walk to Gethsemane with Jesus and His subsequent betrayal and arrest. John 16:33 tells us He said to them, "I have said these things to you, that in me you may have peace. In the world you will have tribulation. But take heart; I have overcome the world."

He warns the disciples about the persecution and suffering they will face as His followers after He leaves. He comforts them with the truth that He will overcome these tribulations with His death and resurrection in the end, but this won't remove them from experiencing hardship of the most brutal variety in the meantime.

He said He would overcome the disciples' trials. That means He will overcome our trials as well, but we still get angry when trials present themselves.

The child repeatedly waking in the night.

The deep exhaustion.

The struggling son or daughter.

The difficult relationship.

The constant barrage of needs.

Why are we so surprised?

We want to blame our trials on the people who seem to cause them, but when do we stop and take a hard look at our role in them? Not very often, or at least not often enough.

Tolerating our own sin and then jumping on everyone else's has never been the way of hope, love, and beauty.

Tolerating our own sin and then jumping on everyone else's has never been the way of hope, love, and beauty.

As I mentioned before, some of our pain is a result of what's done to us, some comes upon us with no earthly explanation, and some we bring on ourselves. My struggles with my daughter are not all her fault; she struggles in ways I may never understand. But my reactions to her have not helped the situation one bit.

What catches me every time I feel upset with a child or I'm mad at myself is that I don't want to live this way. I don't want to be sucked into a cycle of frustration and blaming at every hint of trouble. I want to live lighter, and I want my children to feel and see that. My children deeply experience my disappointment and unhappiness. Even if it's not always about them, it sure feels that way to them. I seem unforgiving and critical of them, and maybe that's because I am.

So many of us walk around hung heavy with guilt and shame because we believe we need to be perfect. Not just better than we are, but perfect. What we always forget, and maybe don't know, is that perfection isn't expected of us. Jesus handed us His perfection as if it were our own.

His perfection was handed to us freely, with great cost to Him and absolutely none to us.

Jesus's perfection was handed to us freely, with great cost to Him and absolutely none to us.

We're expected to come up short. So are the people around us. *That's the whole point.* Imperfection reminds us of our deep need for God—for a Savior. One day God will finish the good work of salvation that He has begun in our hearts, perfecting us. We don't need to get it all right all the time, but we can certainly allow Him the space to work in us, so our lives reflect who He is to us.

30

Procrastinating Like It's My Job

Amanda

The only thing that consoles us for our miseries is distraction, yet that is the greatest of our wretchedness.

Blaise Pascal[1]

A couple of years ago, I read a book called *Eat That Frog*[2] by business expert Brian Tracy. The premise of the book is that if you "eat" the biggest and toughest item on your to-do list first, the rest of the day will be much smoother. It's based on an adage credited to Mark Twain: "Eat a live frog every morning, and nothing worse will happen to you the rest of the day."

I really love that idea, but in my real life it's hard to put into practice, especially since I love box-checking. The more items I can check off in a short amount of time, the better. If I spend an hour taking care of my biggest task first, I can check only one lonely box. *Boo.* But what if that huge job took a bunch of weight off my chest, like making it possible for us to have ongoing insurance coverage or something equally important? Well, now that's worth it. I *think*.

Putting off hard jobs and daunting phone calls feels good for a mere nanosecond, but what feels better is getting them over with. I know that and feel that after I've completed the task, so what makes me want to procrastinate over and over in my everyday life?

The Bible speaks to this—*because of course it does.* These words from Proverbs come to mind: *lazybones, sluggard, fool, slothful, unstable, double minded,* and *idle.* Each one is used to refer to the procrastinators, the lazy, the ones who put off important things. Those words sting so much they practically make my eyes water.

Proverbs also uses words like *diligent, wise, prudent,* and *prospering* to describe people who act on what they need to be doing instead of pushing it off until later. We don't often think of procrastination as sin, but the Bible plainly points out in the New Testament that "whoever knows the right thing to do and fails to do it, for him it is sin" (James 4:17).

Ouch, ouch, ouch. More stinging, more wincing. James is saying putting off the stuff we know we should be doing is sin? Not just a poor choice and crummy use of time, but *sin*?

No wonder procrastination feels so bad. When we're in Christ, our sin makes us feel horrible.

A little mama bird has kept herself super busy beefing up an abandoned nest that sits under the eaves of our covered front porch. She flies away and then back again all day long. She's been at it for weeks. I can't tell if she's about to lay some eggs or if she already has. I'd have to stand on the precarious porch swing to get a peek. But she seems to be preparing for something. Last year, baby birds hatched in that nest, so we're watching and waiting to see if there will be more babies this year. Spring is near, and it's the right time, but how does a bird sense that?

My curious mind always jumps to the deeper questions. How does a bird know her belly is pregnant with eggs? Does it hurt? Is there added pressure she can sense? I don't know, but whatever it is, she gets to work preparing a place of safety for her babies. If she didn't, she'd be in a world of hurt when the time came to deposit her eggs. It makes me laugh to imagine any mama bird not preparing ahead of time and the gossip that might fly around the birdie community as a result.

"You're going to regret sitting back and doing nothing," one mama bird might say to another, scolding it. Maybe that's what's going on when we hear them forcefully tweeting back and forth from the trees. I don't know, but my imagination can't help going there. Are humans the only creatures who wait until the last minute or even forgo finishing their work at all?

I've always been a major procrastinator. I think it stems from my optimistic nature. I'm convinced it will "all be okay" and "work out just fine" no matter what I do or don't do. This attitude serves me well in many areas, but not in any of my current roles. It *does* matter if I get field trip permission slips turned in on time or call to cancel appointments before getting charged for no-shows. Some things can't be put off until tomorrow—or a hundred tomorrows like I keep hoping.

My optimism is seen as a benefit and is pleasing to God when I trust Him to have a handle on what I can't control in my life. And it's good when I can look ahead to my kids' futures that sometimes seem impossibly scary and remember God loves them more than I do and is good to them.

But my optimism becomes a disadvantage when I assume I don't have to do any hard work to improve my relationships, get stuff done, or advance in the areas that are important to me. In addition, optimism weakens me when I place my confidence in my own abilities and strengths. I'm not God, but sometimes being super positive about life leads me to a place of thinking I deserve more authority than I'm meant to have.

For me, procrastination equals misplaced optimism, and sometimes this repetitive cycle leads me to slough off my unfinished work onto someone else's plate, putting unfair pressure on the people around me. My lack of preparation and planning makes them scurry, and I don't like that one bit.

I desperately want to be a woman and mom who can be counted on to follow through and doesn't put off doing what she knows is right and good.

Putting off the hard thing comes in many forms, but for me it looks like finding nearly *anything* to fill my time other than starting dinner or when I don't have the desire to gather the kids together with Jeremy and talk about our faith and read Scripture. Procrastination lingers when the bathrooms need cleaning and a package needs mailing.

Important things often become optional in the fickle recesses of our minds.

Important things often become optional in the fickle recesses of our minds.

The word *fickle* catches me. It's such a weak-sounding description. It makes me think of toddlers and vegetables. When kids don't want to eat the green, orange, or yellow stuff, they're unwilling to yield to what's best for them. The thing is toddlers don't understand all that. All they know is that some vegetables, especially the overcooked and mushy types, are gross.

Keeping with the vegetable analogy, it's impossible for those of us who grew up steeped in American culture to have made it to adulthood without hearing the praises of veggies sung from the rooftops of every TV commercial, health class, and textbook. We know the benefits; there was no way for us to miss them. But important and beneficial things like eating veggies can easily be made into options.

What it comes down to is importance. We must decide what's important enough to benefit from our follow through.

We must decide what's important enough to benefit from our follow through.

31

The Art of Avoidance

Anne-Renee

*Our lives are fashioned by our choices. First we make
our choices. Then our choices make us.*

ANNE FRANK[1]

I sat totally zoned out at a traffic light and let my mind wander aimlessly down a road with stormy clouds to a place of rainbows and grassy pastures. I was yearning for more, but I wasn't sure what more I wanted.

I daydreamed so long that the driver behind me grew restless, honking his disapproval obnoxiously long and loud. As my mind registered the now-green light, it hit me. I was simply going through the motions—of motherhood, of marriage, of ministry. Of life!

I have this bad habit of escapism, finding the art of avoidance more enticing than the feeding and caring of my family. (What? You too?!) As a piano player and someone who fills most of her workday with clicking away at purchase orders, I have found that my fingers itch for something to do when I'm bored. *And ta-da!* My handy little phone that's often right next to me as my copilot, my work assistant, and my text-y friend becomes the perfect evasion tool. A way to escape the chaos and cacophony of motherhood and check out for a while.

Then there's my laptop. I can tuck behind it and completely avoid talking to anyone—for hours (unless bickering begins, which can happen within mere seconds of my fingers touching the keys).

I've been known to choose work and ministry over spending time with my kids. They'll be begging to play a game or read a book together, and there I sit, hands and eyes magnetized to my phone or laptop, repeating phrases like "Give me just two more seconds," "Hold on, please. I'm almost done," and "I'll be right there" over and over, as if on autopilot.

I often wish for bedtime simply to have the house still and carve out some peace and quiet for myself, lamenting, *If only life had a mute button!*

I'll waste big chunks of time doing something completely unnecessary in the moment, trading purposeful minutes with my people for purposeless self-soothing and self-indulgence.

But probably the worst offense of all is that I have this insatiable fondness for scrolling through social media rather than having personal devotions or spending time in God's Word. I mean, who wants conviction when they can have generous pats on the back for a high-ranking post?! A thumbs-up or an emoji heart can speak volumes to this girl desirous of adoration and appreciation.

My mind knows I need discipline, but it yearns to be in the know. Who's doing what. Who's going where. Who's making chili for dinner and who's having chalupas. Like it really matters.

Sadly I have knowingly pushed away my God and my Friend, craving diversion more than craving time with Him.

It's just so crazy easy for me to get out of the rhythm of regularly communicating with the Lord, of seeking Him and looking for answers from His Word. Yes, my wants and my focused attention are two very temperamental things.

I have tried and tried to set up routine practices of healthy spiritual living, but in two seconds' time, I'm distracted. It's like I take one step forward only to leap two digitally enhanced steps back. All it takes for me to jump onto the distraction train is one little side ad popping up while I'm reading my Bible app, and I'm off to see something more appealing, more enticing. Something that'll make me want to push a flashing button to share it with all my friends online.

Yes, I could read my big ol' study Bible rather than reading Scripture online, but the problem is bigger than technology. It has to do with the state of my soul. The yuck that's crept into my heart, encouraging avoidance and breeding laziness.

I'm tired of my prayer life being filled with hollow utterances, always asking for my wants and my needs, and not taking time to listen to God's heart, plans, or desires for me. I'm tired of devotionals and Scripture plans being done halfway and halfheartedly.

So I'm admitting to God, to myself, and to you my avid desire for leisure over doing what I know I should and for choosing the easy way out instead of the path set before me. Because I want change and need to change. How about you?

We are a sinful people, in need of a Savior. As Romans 3:23 says, we have all sinned. We all fall short of His glory. We miss the mark so often. And yet God, because of His marvelous, miraculous love, offers us unwarranted, unmerited, and undeserved amazing grace. Over and over, in the form of Jesus.

So here we are. Back to the choice of what we will fill our days and our minds with. With each new day and each new morning giving us a fresh opportunity and chance to run the race set before us. And to run it well. To direct our focus *on* Him and *for* Him.

Each choice, then, has the option of turning into a practice. And we're always practicing. Forming new habits and continuing old ones—for good, and for bad. Practicing prayer or phone compulsion. Practicing devoted time in the Word or time on social media.

Whether we realize it or not, we are practicing what tomorrow and next week and next year will most likely be if we repeatedly make these same choices.

Of course, the key element to all of this is welcoming in eternal perspective. To make and base our decisions on what is to come. Forming habits that will not only be healthy for us and our families in the now, but gets us into the practice of full living. The kind of full that keeps in mind what the end of life's race will look like. With the Father smiling on as we cross our earthly finish line, our bodies and souls totally beat having used up every ounce of strength to share the gospel of Jesus Christ, excited to hear, "Well done, good and faithful servant" (Matthew 25:21).

We can see it. We can taste it. And our daily practices reflect that future reality, establishing a daily rhythm of being in the Word, of spending time talking (and listening!) to God, of seeing need and responding as the Spirit leads. This is the fruit evident in our lives when our hearts become more like the Father's as He shapes us and trains us.

Yes, this will be difficult and challenging at times, but it's better than checking out and merely going through the motions of living. Or worse yet, wasting valuable life space practicing empty valueless habits.

Don't waste valuable life space practicing valueless habits.

Jesus said, "I came that they may have life and have it abundantly" (John 10:10). He has so much more for us. If we will just stop all this lollygagging and take the time to truly seek it out.

So what will it be? What will we choose?

32

Contentment and the Plain-Jane Everyday

Anne-Renee

*Happiness isn't a destination. It's a journey. And
sometimes the journey is hard.*

Jennifer Dukes Lee[1]

It was late. The kids had been in bed for several hours, and I was in the laundry room folding clothes while waiting for my husband to come home from a long day at work. Clothes that had accumulated into mountains throughout the week filled the tiny space, as though they were fulfilling the biblical command to "be fruitful and multiply."

Resentful notions tossed around in my head, keeping time with the dryer tumbling over and over, until discontentment was the reigning queen of my thoughts.

I wish we didn't live here. If we just moved, everything would be different. I would be so much happier.

As the days turned into weeks and the weeks into months, the mulling continued, and that tiny seed of discontentment grew into a bitter secret garden. It became a place I liked to go and relax every now and again, comforting myself with this cheerful, though false, reality. It felt so cool and inviting there that I began to persuade myself into believing the greenness of the grass in that dreamy state. In that dreamy setting. In that dreamy life.

Ironically, just a few years earlier I was convinced this exact location was where we were called to live and settle down as a family. I had been ready and willing to follow the Lord's leading into this place. I had been purposeful in looking for ways to establish community and sink our roots deep. Where had my elusive, fickle friend Contentment gone?

Sometimes we find ourselves restless in our current season and begin to think that if [fill in the blank] would change, all our wishes could come true. We would, to borrow Elizabeth Bennet's phrase from *Pride and Prejudice*, be "completely, and perfectly, and incandescently happy."[2] If only this utopian place could really exist, filled with never-ending rainbows, happy homes, clean dishes, and obedient children. We yearn for contentment but suppose its location is somewhere other than our current situation or setting. And if you're like me, you find yourself believing that lie—that things will all be better in the future once the present circumstance changes. And that our happiness hinges on that change!

Of course, the enemy of our souls would like to keep us in this exact place of yearning and discontentment. For us to fester and ooze our whinings and woes out onto our families, sharing them with our friends, sowing seeds of "there must be something better out there, something more" wherever we go. Like contagious diseases, unhappiness and disappointment are quick to spread, leaving behind crops of hopelessness and unhealthy hankering.

Oh, how the father of lies must rejoice when we keep ourselves knee-deep in such a swamp, where he can immobilize our thoughts and actions, keeping us from being effective for the kingdom. Where our eyes are fixed only on ourselves and our own needs and wants. Let's be honest. He doesn't want to see us thrive and grow. He doesn't want godly families raised up. And the last thing he wants is for us to conquer our distracted ways and embrace the promised life of victory Jesus offers us.

But praise God! When truth is present, the lies of the Enemy don't stand a chance! No matter the storm, no matter the blah-ness of the day, Christ promises He is with us: "Behold, I am with you always, to the end of the age" (Matthew 28:20).

With the Lord by our side, we can choose blessing amid dissatisfaction: as the psalmist wrote, "I will bless the LORD at all times; his praise shall continually be in my mouth" (Psalm 34:1). In light of such truth, we discover that contentment is not dependent on the state of the situation, but rather an attitude to be chosen. Like the apostle Paul said, "I have learned in whatever situation I am to be content" (Philippians 4:11).

Contentment is not dependent on the state of the situation, but rather an attitude to be chosen.

Maybe it's time to back the truck up and allow God more room to work in our lives. To give Him space to throw in a little game changer here and there. So instead of dwelling on the hollow promises of the mysterious what-could-be, we can begin to see Him in our current circumstances. In our present situations. In our everyday. This is a way of harnessing those daydreams, those yearnings, and those spaces of unhappiness and dissatisfaction and turning them into areas that boost and benefit our growing contentment.

Another way we can do this is to sink our teeth into the promises of God's Word. Seeking out biblical wisdom like a miner digging for gold. Or like a woman in the desert longing for a drink.

As we do this—this searching, digging, and thirsting—our eyes will be opened to seeing His hand. His fingerprints. His workings. Maybe not in the ways we wanted or anticipated, but we can trust God's perfect plan, leaving the end results and outcomes to Him.

As we trust His heart, we begin to grasp and comprehend what

God is using to propel us forward, drawing us to Himself. Those things that prune us and shape us, bringing hope to our families and hope to our souls, helping us become the women He created us to be, for His glory.

In the words of Chrystal Evans Hurst, "Even if we don't have happiness, the Spirit offers us the gift of peace. Like my daddy says, 'Peace doesn't mean you won't have problems. Peace means that your problems won't have you.' While God calls us out of complacency, His peace allows us to choose contentment with our place in the world."[3]

Contentment does not equal complacency. Contentment means resting in the place God presently has you and living there well. Colossians 3:23 says, "Whatever you do, work heartily, as for the Lord."

Contentment doesn't equal complacency. It means resting in the place God presently has you and living there well.

Maybe your heart is bursting with contentment and overflowing with blessing. Maybe you almost skipped this chapter because you don't think this is a problem area for you. Or maybe you're struggling, stuck seeking rest and refuge in your own secret garden of resentment or bitterness.

Wherever you find yourself today, my prayer is that you will find joy in your present circumstances and live today to the very best of your ability—for the honor and glory of our Lord and Savior, Jesus Christ.

It might not be the most comfortable situation to be in, but we can still rest knowing that "he who began a good work in you will bring it to completion at the day of Christ Jesus" (Philippians 1:6).

Rest there, Mom. In His capable hands is a good place to be.

All the Good Things

Overcoming the Just Don't Wannas

To Remember

- Each day brings a new set of chances for us to react in a God-honoring way to the life and people we've been given.
- Important things often become optional in the fickle recesses of our minds.
- Don't waste valuable life space practicing valueless habits.
- Contentment is not dependent on the state of the situation, but rather an attitude to be chosen.
- We can rest, knowing that in His capable hands is a good place to be.

To Hold On To

I came that they may have life and have it abundantly (John 10:10).

I have learned in whatever situation I am to be content (Philippians 4:11).

Whatever you do, work heartily, as for the Lord (Colossians 3:23).

To Consider

Choose a healthy habit you'd like to grow in and find a friend who'd like to join you.

- Be consistent. Keep it simple. Avoid excuses.
- Give each other grace when you fail, and then get up and start again.

Part Nine

The Me I Want To Be

Who I Am When the WiFi Goes

Amanda

I am beginning to learn that it is the sweet,
simple things of life which are the real ones after all.

LAURA INGALLS WILDER[1]

In the fall of 2017, major hurricanes Harvey, Irma, and Maria hit Texas, Florida, and Puerto Rico (as well as the neighboring islands) with a vengeance. They brought insane amounts of rain and wind, resulting in horrific flooding and damage that devastated thousands upon thousands of families with the loss of homes and livelihoods. Many lost their lives.

We followed Harvey's destruction the most closely since we have friends who lived in its direct path in Texas. We watched the water rise to and into their houses as the storm moved over them. We watched it destroy their neighborhoods as they captured the event on social media with update after update.

One of the families had just moved into their brand-new home one week earlier. It was unreal. She was posting pictures and commenting about how much work it was to unpack while still doing family life with her husband and three girls, and then the very next week their entire downstairs was ruined by flood waters that rose several feet right in their new kitchen and living areas. Parts of Houston and many other parts of South Texas seemed to be completely underwater.

I've never lived through a major natural disaster of that kind, but what I observed from a distance didn't surprise me in the least. People came together to help one another, as is usual when disaster strikes. Getting ahead, cocooning in their own busy lives, and continuing business as usual weren't options. They pulled together and acted as one big unit, so they could get to the other side of calamity without losing too much more than they already had.

It seems to take a disaster for most of humankind to stop long enough to see other people.

Shortly after hurricane Irma hit Florida, a man who lived through the storm shared his experiences:

> The most amazing thing happened Sunday morning when the storm died down—everyone came outside. It was part disaster tourism, part curiosity, and part "Hey, you guys okay?"
>
> By my count, roughly two-thirds of the neighborhood was outside, and there was a lot of conversation. We seized this small window of time to meet numerous "new" neighbors and have several substantive conversations. We talked about adoption with some neighbors considering it. We had fireside s'mores with discussions on faith and science. We got to hear people's stories and share our own...
>
> After my experience, I'm increasingly convinced that two of the biggest barriers to neighborly living are air conditioning and the internet. When stripped of these two luxuries, people were forced to interact as embodied persons. The multitude of distractions available on the internet were simply gone.[2]

When our flow of information and comfort is interrupted, we change directions. In this case, the people turned to each other. Once out of their shelters and in the calm after the storm, the people met neighbors they'd never spoken to and had real, face-to-face conversations. They had no air conditioning to keep them inside and no internet to keep them distracted.

How quickly circumstances—even after such a difficult event—changed for the better. Thousands of people had just survived a hurricane, and the damage was evident, but here were these same people living their best life, the way humankind was intended to live. Together. Dependent on one another. Knowing one another.

Who would I be as a person and mother with no WiFi or data plans? Who would you be without the comforts that keep us so separated?

One Saturday afternoon when I was in search of a bit of quiet, I told the kids I was going outside and not to follow me. I not only needed peace, but I also needed some fresh air and head space for ten minutes or so. I took my journal and a bag of one of my newer vices, plantain chips, and headed down the driveway to first check the mail. My phone stayed inside on the kitchen counter, where it probably should stay more often.

I took several deep breaths along the way, filling my lungs to capacity each time. I've been trying to be more mindful of my breathing and stop to take several deep breaths a day. (Are you taking shallow breaths right now? Try pausing to take a deep breath. Or two or several more. It helps, no?)

Checking the mail is a simple thing that makes me way too happy, and this time didn't disappoint. I shoved the package, Costco magazine, and a couple of letters into my already full arms and started walking around the other side of our circle drive along the creek and toward the house.

Then I saw her—the fluffy, black stray cat who had been frequenting our yard. She was pregnant and skittish, and I kept trying to woo her to myself like one of the toddlers at church I'm always trying to befriend.

She was sniffing at our basement door and looking through the glass when I spotted her. I took that to mean she wanted to live with us forever. I followed her around to the other side of the house as she warily stared at me and then moved whenever I got anywhere close to her. I even held out a plantain chip, but she didn't buy it.

Then she crawled under our neighbor's raised shed, and I stood on our property line, calling her with my arms still full. I moved away when I saw my neighbor pull into her driveway. We're new around here, and I didn't want her to think me too strange for staring at her shed. I walked back to our front steps and sat for a while, brainstorming how I'd get this cat to trust me.

Cat bed? Food? A safe place to have her babies? Hmm. All the above? After pondering for a while, I went back inside.

Those few minutes held nothing spectacular, and I didn't write in my journal or even eat any plantain chips, but I felt like myself. My zany, optimistic, simplicity and joy-seeking self. No electricity required—just everyday wonder that's always there if I take the time to enjoy it.

What other everyday wonders am I missing when I have my head down, stuck in distracting patterns? (Way more than is necessary.) What might I be missing because of the way I'm living right now?

I haven't seen the cat again, but I did spend four dollars on a small bag of cat food and made her a little bed out of a cardboard box and an old towel and set it out with some food and water. Jeremy and the kids rolled their eyes, of course. But they also loved it. I'm taking the time to be fully myself, and they appreciate that.

I should too.

Why are these moments of truly being ourselves so rare if we enjoy them so much? What is keeping us from this kind of enjoyment, this kind of simplicity?

For me, the problem is time-wasting of various kinds and social media. Do these things bring any benefit to me? Well, sure. And when I take a little break, it's beneficial for my family as well as for me. But I must ask myself if I really need several "little" (or not so little) breaks all day long? Do I need to check in, check in, check in until I don't like myself anymore? And by not like myself, I mean hate myself for wasting so much time?

Real life is waiting, and it's not inside the screen I'm staring at. Real people in my life, both "out there" and inside my own home, are lonely and waiting for someone to invest in them. But because I'm otherwise occupied, they're spending their moments another way. They miss out, and so do I. I have neighbors to meet, birds to listen to, leaves to crunch underfoot, conversations to have, smiles to give, and silence to enjoy.

Who would you be without WiFi? Be her.

Who would you be without WiFi? Be her.

P.S.—It took the cat a while to eat the first round of food I set out, but once she realized it was available for the taking, she came back again and again, and she continues to do so. She usually comes in the darkness of night, I'm sure to avoid the ten humans who live here.

34

The Regret of Lost Time

Amanda

How did it get so late so soon?

Dr. Seuss[1]

One of my greatest, looming concerns in all of parenting is that Jeremy and I will get to the end of the time we had with each of our kids at home and realize we wasted so much of it. That we will have left out necessary life lessons and instead crammed in loads of meaningless clamor, all the while walking around exhausted and lifeless with little to no motivation for truly pouring into them in the ways they needed most.

My three oldest are teenagers, and I'm feeling this concern bigtime. The years go by slowly when you're raising kids (we all know that's the truth no matter what the grocery store lady says about their going fast), but the number of years we have with them *is* relatively short. When you consider the whole span of a human life, 18 years with your kids doesn't seem that long.

I love my teens—they're great kids I sincerely enjoy being around. They have their sin struggles just like everyone else, and we're working on areas with each of them, but I think they're going to be okay. *Okay*, however, is relative. How my kids turn out is not just about their behavior and how they act. Who they become is based mostly on how they think and where they put their hope. This outlook will drive all their actions.

The question I ask myself when our parenting seems focused on the wrong things is this: *Have I taught my kids how to think properly and biblically about God, themselves, and the world?*

Isn't this our most important aim in parenting? To teach our kids the most important things in life, which, as Christians, is teaching them about God's love for us and salvation for them in Jesus Christ? They need to know God offers Jesus's sinless record in exchange for ours, so we can be with Him forever in heaven and glorify Him always.

That, of course, is easier to type out on a keyboard or read in a book than to live out in real life, passing it on to our kids as the ultimate truth.

I didn't grow up learning catechisms (a word that in the Greek simply means, "to teach orally") and I've only recently started learning about them. Catechisms are series of questions and answers recited aloud and memorized to help both children and adults know and understand the major principles of the Christian faith. After dinner, and for the next couple of years, our family is working our way through *The New City Catechism*[2], going through its 52 questions and answers to help us better understand our faith and live it out. We each have our own tiny booklet, and we're all benefiting from learning this way. This is new for every one of us, so no one is more "schooled" in it than another. It's great.

This routine stems from the nagging feeling I've had in the pit of my stomach as a mom, the feeling that something needs to change or it's going to be too late. Our family never misses a Sunday at church, we pray together before meals, and we filter life through the lens of the gospel. Our faith and passing it along are important to Jeremy and me, and looking in from the outside, all looks fine—exemplary, even. But we know that's not the case.

We've been lacking in passing along our real, everyday faith and the processing of it. We've been talking *at* our kids about faith instead of talking *with* them about faith. There's a significant difference, but it's so subtle we'll miss it if we aren't paying attention. Some of the people closest to us might be tempted to argue with me here, saying that what they see us doing is anything but lacking. But we know our hearts. We've become extremely tired and lax. It's easy to talk about faith rather than truly engage with our kids about it. To preach it, but not practice it.

Our children's faith decision isn't dependent on us, but their first introduction usually begins with us and is cultivated through the years as we teach and encourage them in it. All the responsibility for our kids' faith doesn't fall on us, but some of it certainly does.

The journey Moses and the Israelites took to enter the promised land, the land called Canaan, is chronicled in the Old Testament books of Exodus, Numbers, Deuteronomy, and Joshua. This was the destination God guaranteed the nation of Israel through Abraham 430 years before Moses and the Israelite slaves fled Egypt and the Egyptian dynasty that had enslaved them (Exodus 14).

With Moses as their leader, the whole nation of Israel was then sentenced to wander the desert for 40 years because their hearts repeatedly became rebellious after God rescued them from their captors. When this massive group finally reached the border of Canaan and their years of roaming ended, Moses wasn't permitted to take them into the promised land because of his disobedience in an incident with the rock and waters of Meribah (Numbers 20:6-12).

That part of the story has always been hard for me to comprehend. Moses led the people so well those 40 years! I think this would be akin to us raising our kids with all the hardship and joy and exhaustion that goes with it (give or take a million children like Moses "parented"), and then not being able to be in their lives past age 18. We wouldn't get to walk with them through the rest of their days. It breaks my heart just thinking about it.

But that was the position Moses was in, the position all the Israelites who were in that first generation of people present at the exodus were in. None of them were permitted to enter the land set apart for them, to walk with their descendants into God's promise for them. Their unfaithfulness to God excluded everyone except Caleb and Joshua. Because of their wholehearted devotion to God, they were the only ones from the exodus generation to be allowed entrance. Joshua was named the successor to Moses, the one who would lead them over the Jordan River and into the land they were to possess.

This feels confusing and sad—unfair, even—but a holy God desires holiness from His people, and He knew what was best in the end for the Israelites, and for Moses. *Whew*—Moses had a tough assignment. How he held it together, I'll never know. If I had been responsible for everything he was responsible for all those years, I probably would have committed a few crimes against those disobedient, idol-worshipping people.

Right before approximately two and a half million Israelites crossed over the Jordan River and into Canaan, Moses had some words for them on the plains of Moab. He was preparing his people before they moved into the next phase of the journey without him. He was also trying to redirect their eyes heavenward.

The book of Deuteronomy is his final speech. From the start of the book all the way up until his death, Moses reminded the next generation of Israelites of all the laws given by God to their forefathers, along with the blessings for obedience and consequences for disobedience. It was his parting message, probably a lot like what we'd give to our children if we had one last chance to speak to them: "Do [this] and don't do [that] so it will go well with you, and most importantly, devote yourselves to God and pass it down to your children."

For our purposes, to beef up our parental priorities, we're going to look at the instructions Moses gave to the parents and future parents of Israel in Deuteronomy 6:4-9. They captivate me every time I read this passage because it lays out God's plan for us in a way we can understand:

> Hear, O Israel: The LORD our God, the LORD is one. You shall love the LORD your God with all your heart and with all your soul and with all your might. And these words that I command you today shall be on your heart. You shall teach them diligently to your children, and shall talk of them when you sit in your house, and when you walk by the way, and when you lie down, and when you rise. You shall bind them as a sign on your hand, and they shall be as frontlets between your eyes. You shall write them on the doorposts of your house and on your gates.

His main points were:

- Listen to and obey these words.
- Recognize God as the only living and true God.
- Love Him with everything in you.
- Carry these words close.
- Teach them to your children and talk about them always.
- Keep them at the forefront of your minds and surroundings.

Even more succinctly, Moses was encouraging them to:

- Honor God.
- Obey Him willingly.
- Love Him fully.

- Then pass all this down to their children and grandchildren.

I love short lists. My *ooh-shiny* mind needs instructions to be brief and to the point.

Moses was the first prophet to foretell the coming of a Savior—the Messiah, Jesus Christ. And interestingly, Moses was the only prophet Jesus was ever compared to (Hebrews 3). Jesus is found to be much greater than Moses, but you have to love how Moses was honored by its author. Moses was a faithful man. Sinful yes, but he also loved God and consistently taught and trained the younger generations.

The life of Moses encourages me so much as I parent my crew. But the one thing Moses missed is Jesus. The Israelites then did not have salvation through Jesus, nor the indwelling of the Holy Spirit. But *we* do. And that's the other important component, the most important component of our teachings as parents. If we impart our knowledge of and belief in Jesus as the One who will never let down our kids, we've done exactly what God is asking of us. And if our kids choose to embrace Jesus and the gospel as their own? Well, throw the biggest party, because that's the best news in all of parenting.

Let's look at some of Jesus's last words to His followers after His death on the cross and His resurrection, just He went back to heaven.

> The eleven disciples went to Galilee, to the mountain to which Jesus had directed them. And when they saw him they worshiped him, but some doubted. And Jesus came and said to them, "All authority in heaven and on earth has been given to me. Go therefore and make disciples of all nations, baptizing them in the name of the Father and of the Son and of the Holy Spirit, teaching them to observe all that I have commanded you. And behold, I am with you always, to the end of the age" (Matthew 28:16-20).

This is another one of those *final instruction* type passages. First, we saw one from Moses, and now we see one from Jesus. In addition to what Moses said, Jesus stressed the importance of making disciples, of multiplying ourselves by telling what we know and have seen.

What do we know to be true of God from His Word?

What do we know to be true of God from our own experiences?

Let's go and share those things. We'll never regret it.

35

I Don't Want to Be a Tripping Hazard

Anne-Renee

Lord, make me an instrument of your peace:
where there is hatred, let me sow love;
where there is injury, pardon;
where there is doubt, faith;
where there is despair, hope;
where there is darkness, light;
where there is sadness, joy.

PRAYER OF SAINT FRANCIS OF ASSISI

I played the garbled message on our answering machine and tried not to sigh too audibly as I listened to its request. The gal scheduled to play piano on Sunday morning was battling the flu, and our music pastor needed a sub. Would I be willing to fill in for both services? My head hung low. I'd been looking forward to sleeping in a little later on Sunday, but now I was going to have to get up bright and early and go serve the Lord!

I don't know how many times I've heard about someone needing help and I've wracked my brain to think of someone else to help them. Someone with fewer things on their plate. Someone stronger, better equipped, or with more resources. I have given myself excuse after excuse why I shouldn't physically be the one to come to their aid.

But what arrogance! Is my time worth more than someone else's? Are my resources more precious or more valuable? Is the emotional or physical cost greater for me than it would be for someone else? And do I honestly believe God would ask me to serve Him without equipping me to do it?

Most of the time, when thinking through and weighing out the options for giving relief and support, I come to the head-scratching conclusion that I probably should help—if I could just clear my schedule and shift a few things. (Read this last sentence verrrry sloooowly. Imagine Eeyore reading it, and you'll detect my sense, or lack thereof, of urgency.)

In my hesitation, though, often someone else steps up to fill the need, some servant who reacts quickly to the Spirit's promptings without giving the Lord every excuse under the sun for why they can't lend a hand.

This habit has become more than a dragging of feet, as we talked about in chapter 31, "The Art of Avoidance." This is a blatant putting off whatever calls me out of what's comfortable. Anything inconvenient, unknown, or overwhelming. A choosing of what is easy and effortless rather than being willing to wade into the deep.

This is an admitted area of weakness for me. A quandary of choosing selfishness over selflessness. Time and failure have taught me that the first step outside of a comfort zone is often the hardest one to take. Excuses must be pushed aside. Anxieties must be quieted. And selfishness must take a seat. Preferably the last one in the room.

The first step outside of your comfort zone is often the hardest one to take.

In the book of Luke, we're introduced to an amazing cast of friends, all-star comrades who were quite the opposite of selfish in terms of knowingly going into hard places. These friends were fearless. Totally willing to go the extra mile for a friend in need. Even if it meant making a scene, cutting ceiling tiles, and interrupting a sermon to get him in front of Jesus. Who just happened to be the keynote speaker!

Everyone was there, from Galilee to Judea and Jerusalem. It was a supersized gathering, and with the magnitude of the crowd, these friends couldn't even get through with their precious cargo—a man so paralyzed, he had to travel on his bed. Yet they were unfazed by the number of people crowded around the Master. When the throngs of people pushed in harder and they couldn't get through, they decided on a plan B. They were persistent and unstoppable.

Now, there's some debate on the roofing material mentioned in the book of Luke because tiles weren't widely used during that time period. The average roof consisted of slabs of mud laid out to bake and harden in the sun. However, Luke clearly states that they "went up on the roof and let him down with his bed through the tiles into the midst before Jesus" (Luke 5:19). It's possible that this home belonged to someone quite wealthy who could afford a tile roof. Or maybe the house belonged to some elite contractor trying out the latest and greatest in roofing.

All material options aside, letting someone down through a roof was serious business, serious enough to be highlighted in this story along with the paralyzed man's faith and the faith of his loyal friends: "When [Jesus] saw their faith, he said, 'Man, your sins are forgiven you'" (Luke 5:20).

That's the kind of friend I want to be! A woman willing to do whatever it takes to lead and urge those around me to the feet of Jesus. A woman who wants to help even when it's inconvenient, when it's out of my comfort zone, or when I don't remotely feel like it. I want to be the kind of friend who comes alongside a hurting sister, and who will hold fast and hold firm even when muscles are burning and about to give way from the weight of the load. Physically and prayerfully holding her up. Fueled with the purpose of getting that girl to the healing presence of our Lord and Savior. Because that's what a real friend would do—carting her to Jesus and helping her carry on when life has paralyzed her on every side.

This fresh perspective on friendship not only allows me to be a better friend, but also frees me from all the twisted, tangled-up notions I have about what sisterhood truly means. It permits me to love my family of faith and those outside that family with a Christlike love. It's an active affection that cares, provides, protects, assists, bends over backward and forward, and loves no matter what.

It's a never-gonna-give-up kind of devotion. An *I'm going to step out of my comfort zone and into the mess with you* manner of love. It's willing to go deep and pray hard. To get messy and cheer another on. It's accountability, encouragement, and being that iron that sharpens iron (Proverbs 27:17), even when it's uncomfortable or seems like the worst possible timing. And because we're not responsible for the replenishing of this kind of love, it can run on grace and be refueled by a spirit of compassion—all because of Jesus.

There is no requirement for perfection or expectation for dramatic results. It's simply a love willing to show up no matter what, to carry a sister or brother, and to do whatever it takes to lessen another's load.

Listing It Is Easier Than Living It

Anne-Renee

The day will be what you make it, so rise, like the sun, and burn.
WILLIAM C. HANNAN[1]

You know the line in the old Christmas song, "Santa Claus Is Coming to Town" about checking your list twice?

I've always loved that lyric because I love making lists. For Christmas baking and Christmas gifts. For daily to-dos and grocery needs. For work priorities and purchasing tasks. For school supply shopping and summer camping necessities. I love to see nice neat rows of items organized and put into feasible steps—specifically, lists jam-packed with specifics and practical application. If each item has a petite check box cozied up next to it, all the better. Checking a little square box makes my heart sing.

So when it comes to listing out priorities to keep me focused, I'm all about it. Give me a cutesy pocket-sized notebook and a favorite pen, and I'll write the heck out of that list. I will number them. Alphabetize them. I will even color code them in order of importance if you really want me to. Because order translates as beauty to this brain of mine.

Listing out priorities is so much easier than actually having to live them out. Like day to day. Hour to hour. Minute by minute. It's far less complicated to list something than live something.

Listing it out is easier than living it out.

I can give you all sorts of reasons why I like to do something. For example, I could give you song and verse of all the ways I enjoy showing love to my family or enjoy serving within my home church. But if I never do any of those things, if I never live them out, what good is it to list them? A list of priorities is only as valuable as the life defined and transformed by them.

A list of priorities is only as valuable as the life defined and transformed by them.

I'm not saying we shouldn't write out goals or resolutions. But the list shouldn't stop at the writing phase. It needs someone to come alongside it and make it possible. For feasibility to take a firm hand and guide that priority into fruitful culmination and completion. So if we've pushed aside the things that birth distraction and we're wholeheartedly seeking what the Lord would have us do in our everyday lives, there is a natural sifting of sorts that needs to take place. An assessing and weighing, a pondering and evaluating. A deliberate pushing aside of that which is not helpful in our daily walk, and choosing to pursue that which urges us Godward.

Our priorities are what is left at the end of this sorting process, revealing the things we value the most and want to take precedence in our lives.

And so we list them. We put objectives to paper and purpose to the test, naming those areas and ways we want to move forward and connect action steps to our good intentions.

But it is the living. The breathing. The acting out of our principles that makes a difference. Ultimately, the proof is found in the out-come, or as the old proverb goes, "The proof of the pudding is in the eating." The end result exposes the effectiveness of the practical application.

We can chat all we want about loving and serving others, but if we never put loving and serving into practice, we're just broadcast-ing hollow noise, teeming with lots of talk and devoid of action. First Corinthians 13:1 gives us further insight into this reality: "If I speak in the tongues of men and of angels, but have not love, I am a noisy gong or a clanging cymbal."

This is a pretentious way of living, saying we're going to act a certain way, giving others the impression that we're going to do something but then never doing it. We're merely making empty commotion, a pointless hullabaloo with no substance behind our words or worth behind our actions. It's a duplicitous way of living.

Frankly, the more I contemplate the fragility of our days here on earth, the more I come to the conclusion that life is way too short to fill it up with meaningless stuff. Like you, I want my life to count for something, for love to be the foundation of all these blessed ideologies floating around my mind and bursting off my tongue. I don't want to just talk about being God-focused; I want to live that way.

But in order for priorities to become a priority, we must leave behind self-gratification, laziness, and mediocrity. To give preference to grace and compassion over indifference and complacency. That can be hard. And uncomfortable. And downright tough to push aside that which soothes and pacifies our self-righteousness and self-cen-teredness. To put into action that wholehearted trust in our great God, allowing His living, breathing Spirit to dominate our mind and our actions.

When perspective is in question and I'm not sure what my next step should be, I look at what's going on in the news. Somehow terrorist attacks, shootings, political upheaval, and natural disasters help to realign my priorities and adjust uncertain points of view.

Take today's news, for instance. NBC News just announced that 305 people were killed while praying in a mosque in Egypt. Twenty-seven were children.[2] A giant lump forms in my throat as I look out my dining room window and see my children laughing and squealing in the snow—while the reality and weight of God's sovereignty once again crashes into my questioning heart.

I don't understand the pain. The devastation. The senselessness.

As the kiddos pile into the house with wet mittens and red noses, I gather them in my arms to pray. We stop, acknowledging the aching world and petitioning the gates of heaven for mercy, then we hug long and tight. And like forgetful, playful puppies, they shift gears and giggle their way into the kitchen to make cookies while I stay in the dining room a little while longer, watching the swirling snow and pondering my place in this crazy world.

Author Shannan Martin describes it like this: "[God] offers the opportunity to experience a richness we'd never know if we remained locked in the prison of our false security and maximized agendas. Here, in our everyday, he invites us in to the abundant life."[3]

So for today, my priorities look like this:

- Lay a foundation of prayerful trust for our family.
- Invite thankfulness in.
- Make our home a place of peace.
- Pray for those hurting from heartbreaking loss.
- Ask the Lord what it means for us to practically live out the good news today.

Doing these things may not feel like much, and yet, for me, they are an act of obedience. A simple trust. A resting in His God-ness.

Deep down I know God doesn't need me to be about His business, but He wants me to be. And for today, that's what I must remember—to keep my eyes fixed on Him. No, I can't mend all the world's problems, but I can do my best to be a part of the solution, one priority and prayer at a time.

All the Good Things

The Me I Want to Be

To Remember

- Real life is waiting, and it's not inside the screen we're staring at.
- We must ask ourselves this question: *Have I taught my kids how to think properly and biblically about God, themselves, and the world?*
- The first step outside our comfort zone is often the hardest one to take.
- A list of priorities is only as valuable as the life defined and transformed by them.

To Hold On To

> Jesus came and said to them, "All authority in heaven and on earth has been given to me. Go therefore and make disciples of all nations, baptizing them in the name of the Father and of the Son and of the Holy Spirit, teaching them to observe all that I have commanded you. And behold, I am with you always, to the end of the age" (Matthew 28:18-20).

> I am sure of this, that he who began a good work in you will bring it to completion at the day of Jesus Christ (Philippians 1:6).

To Consider

- Who would you be without WiFi or a data plan? List three ways you'd be different.

- Choose a distraction to fast from this week and see how it affects your mothering.

Part Ten

Beyond Shiny

Making Them Feel Different

Amanda

Whether we are in crisis or chaos or calm, hope or disappointment,
burial or resurrection, ordinary or extraordinary, we can—
because of the inexhaustible grace of God—begin again.

LEANNA TANKERSLEY[1]

When I was eight years old, my family took a giant leap and moved to Alaska. I had never even visited there before arriving in the middle of all that snow and ice. I was convinced we'd be living in an igloo and entertaining pet penguins. Thankfully, once we arrived, I saw that people there live in real houses and learned penguins live only south of the equator.

We were starting all over in Alaska, but little did I know what starting over would come to mean. Two years after settling into our new life, my parents divorced. I don't remember the fights leading up to it, but I do remember moments of explosive anger from my dad. I remember that so well.

But who my dad is now is who I know him to be. He has long since changed, and that's so, so good. When I look at him, I don't see someone who had angry outbursts in the past; I see my supportive, kind, and healed father. He's the guy who gets choked up on the phone when we're about to hang up now that we live in different states. I see and love who he is now with no bitterness attached.

That's the way God sees and loves us. He redeems our past failures to make them an integral part of the larger story He's weaving. It's all useful and all redeemable. If we've had bad moments, bad seasons, or bad years, we can move past them and be different. Jesus makes us whole again when we go to Him in humility and repentance.

Not only that, but we can help bring healing and wholeness to the people we've hurt, pushed aside, and ignored with our actions and words. It's important that we speak to those people, especially our children, to help them move forward as well. If we push for our own healing and never look back to remember whom we've harmed, then the process won't feel complete.

If we push for our own healing and never look back to remember whom we've harmed, then the process won't feel complete.

This makes me think of the apostle Paul and his conversion story in the book of Acts. Paul, who previously went by Saul, was a devout Jew, a Pharisee who thought he was doing what was called for as a vicious persecutor of Christians. He was punishing those he thought were blaspheming God the Father by following Jesus of Nazareth, who he didn't believe was the promised Messiah.

Paul was first mentioned in the Bible at the stoning of Stephen (Acts 7:54-60), the first person martyred for believing in Jesus. Saul approved of the murder of Stephen and stood by and watched him being pummeled with great satisfaction. Acts 8 goes on to chronicle the horrors Saul inflicted on the church as he dragged believers from their homes and threw them in prison.

He was feared far and wide, and no one could have guessed what would happen next.

Acts 9 opens with Saul traveling to Damascus on foot to continue his pursuit and horrific treatment of Christians. That's when Jesus met him with a bright light from heaven that left him blind for three days. Saul didn't see Jesus, but he certainly heard His voice.

Acts 9:4-6 tells us, "Falling to the ground, he heard a voice saying to him, 'Saul, Saul, why are you persecuting me?' And he said, 'Who are you, Lord?' And he said, 'I am Jesus, whom you are persecuting. But rise and enter the city, and you will be told what you are to do.'"

After this, Saul was led by hand to Damascus, where he stayed, still blinded and neither eating nor drinking. Meanwhile, Jesus visited a believer named Ananias in a vision, telling him to go find Saul (the man with the awful and scary reputation) and put his hand on him to bring healing that would restore his sight. Three days after the blinding light on the road to Damascus, Saul was visited by Ananias, and his vision was restored just as the Lord said. He was filled with the Holy Spirit and baptized, and he spent time with the Christ followers in Damascus before beginning his public ministry.

He started using the name Paul, a Roman name rather than his previous Greek name, probably to signify his new nature in Christ and to prepare for his future work in Rome. Whatever the exact reason, he is referred to as Paul in the rest of the Bible, from Acts 13:9 on.

Raise your hand if you thought Jesus changed Paul's name. Yep, me too. I guess I never realized he just decided to start going by Paul. Thanks, childhood Sunday school, or, well, maybe it was just me.

Paul's conversion story is important for us to keep in mind. It shows us what God can do with the most impossible situations and most unlikely people. God loves to use unlikely people in impossible situations for His matchless glory.

What do we remember Paul for? What marks his life in our minds? His latter missionary work and the colossal impact he had in the world for Christ, no question.

This brings me back to us. I love Paul's story because it further proves the notion that we'll be remembered for who we are starting now, more than who we've been in the past.

We'll be remembered for who we are starting now, more than who we've been in the past.

Recently, a journalist visited Tonya Harding, the former champion figure skater who is most known for a scandal. In January 1994, rival American skater Nancy Kerrigan was clubbed on the leg by an assailant.[2] He was a hitman of sorts, hired by Tonya's ex-husband to injure Nancy enough that she'd be forced to withdraw from the Olympic Games in Lillehammer, Norway, scheduled for the following month.

The injury Nancy sustained wasn't enough to keep her from competing at the Games, and in a Lifetime-movie-worthy turn of events, both she and Tonya were selected to represent the United States in the Ladies Singles event.

I remember the stress I felt watching them practice on the ice at the same time before the competition began. It was so awkward and tense as they steered clear of eye contact and tried their best to focus on the job at hand, rather than on the drama the world was now zeroed in on.

Nancy Kerrigan went on to win the silver medal, and Tonya placed eighth in the final standings. Do you remember that scene where Tonya was crying about her faulty shoelace, begging for a re-skate, her leg and skate kicked up on the boards in front of the judges? It was all part of the drama.

The men involved in Nancy Kerrigan's attack served time in prison, and because evidence showed Tonya was also involved in the incident (although she avoided legal sentencing), she was eventually banned from any future involvement with U.S. Figure Skating.

The journalist who interviewed Tonya for the *New York Times* article handled her job with tact and grace, and I appreciated that when I read it. I'll never forget the compassion she showed Tonya in the article once she realized and stated she was displaying the same attributes many people who have lived through trauma display. Tonya's trauma was a tumultuous childhood and toxic relationships.

I always want to look for the best in people and have compassion for where they came from and why they behave the way they do. That's important for sure as we mother our own people, but we can take into our mothering another important aspect from Tonya's story. This is my reason for bringing her into this chapter.

If you remember that incident and all that followed, what comes to mind when you think of Tonya Harding? I think of words like *sneaky*, *untrustworthy*, and *conniving*. I don't claim any of those to be godly thoughts or even true descriptions of her. But why do I—and maybe you as well—have words like that in my head 20-plus years after the fact?

I think I know why: because Tonya has yet to make me feel differently about her with her actions. All these years later my thoughts about her are still mostly connected to that incident in 1994, not to anything she's done since that could change my mind.

While all of this is hard to stomach because I'm not a fan of thinking poorly of someone, nor do I think it's pleasing to God when we do, this reality gives me great hope. Let me explain:

This reminds me of what happened the other morning when I got the five younger kids up and ready for school. Jeremy and I usually tag-team these mornings, but on that day he was sleeping in because he'd been working into the wee hours. When my alarm went off at 6:10 a.m., I prayed God would help me get all the kids off to school with kindness, patience, and no sign of irritability.

As we all know, mornings can be tricky, and I wanted to be stronger than tricky can make me. I wanted Christ in me to be what moved me and led me through the motions of getting them dressed and fed, with teeth brushed, hair done, and shoes, coats, and backpacks on.

Despite my inner preparation and vow to do better, however, my very first interaction with one of my kids sent me through the roof. I felt so frustrated and defeated that I bawled the whole time I was getting them ready and loading up for the drive to school. I was mad at myself for reacting the way I did, and I was mad at my child for being so difficult so often. On the short drive, I made it right with my child, and then I asked forgiveness from the whole van load for the scene I caused and for the way I'd reacted.

My kids saw my frailty as a person that morning, yes, but they saw Jesus in the way I forgave. Our children see our failures *for sure*, but they also have a chance to see our forgiveness and humility. That's like Him too.

We can behave differently from this moment on, so the memories people have of us are pleasant. We can repent of our past actions, like Paul, and move forward in love and humility.

That's the gift we can give in this moment, right here.

38

This Moment Right Here

Amanda

What we do now echoes in eternity.

MARCUS AURELIUS

Sometimes I play this little game with myself. I guess you could call it "try not to give the kids another embarrassing story to tell people about me when they're grown-ups." Do you ever play that?

What will they say about me when they're sitting around with their friends in college or with their husbands or wives or even our grandkids someday? What will they make fun of me for? Which of my mess-ups will they talk about?

Yet I guess I'm not as afraid they'll tell stories about my embarrassing mess-ups as I'm afraid that I'm going to mess *them* up and will have squandered the years I had with them. I'm afraid the stories will be about that.

What will my children say was most important to me when they look back on their growing-up years? Will it be my love and commitment to God, my family, and people all those years, or will it be order, silence, box checking, their obedience, my appearance, phones, screens, and perfection? Oh, how I wish it didn't matter how I spend my days, that my kids would automatically have everything they need and learn every important thing despite how I manage myself and my time. But that's simply not the case.

What will my children say was most important to me when they look back on their growing-up years?

When we stop long enough to really think about it, our true desire as mothers isn't just getting through each day with our kids; it's raising them to love God, love people, and live their lives in pursuit of these most important things. If we could tack on a bit more, we'd love for them to eventually be wonderful people who positively contribute to society and the world for Christ, and to be people we enjoy being around later. *Please let us enjoy being around them later.*

Worrying doesn't make any of that happen, but aren't we good at worrying instead of doing what we can to make each moment better, to work toward those goals?

I had a delightfully disturbing realization this year that helped me ease the burden I was carrying about what my children would take from their years living with me. The kids and I were sitting around talking about books, and I said, "Hey, do you guys remember when I read you that chapter book about the family who moved from the city to the country and learned to tap the trees for maple syrup? It was so good!"

After reading it aloud to them, I bought taps for the trees in our yard, so we could eventually make birch syrup from our spindly Alaskan trees. It all felt so quaint and cozy.

The kids all shook their heads no. They had zero recollection of the four plus months we'd spent reading that book. And apparently, they didn't remember any of the other books I'd read to them during those younger years either. Hmm. I'd spent all that time for them, and with them.

It was disturbing, yes. But when I really thought about it, I realized it was wonderful that they didn't remember! Their memory blank was good news to me. It meant they didn't remember every one of my screw-ups either. I could see that what I'm stressing over right now about the kids and my certain lacking mom skills don't matter as much as I think they do or even should.

We can be so hard on ourselves for not doing all the wonderful things we think we should be doing. When I'm in a negative mind-set about myself, I categorize our circumstances in one of two ways: (1) a death sentence that will never lift or (2) a brief calm before the next storm. I assume my kids will take away some kind of wound or come up short in some way, even from things I can't change.

For the most part, I'm wrong about that. Kids are extremely resilient and forgiving, more than we usually give them credit for. The fact that they didn't remember something we spent so much time on was extremely freeing for me. Truly, even though reading that book and all the follow-up activities are something I'd be happy for them to remember me by.

When we focus on everything that's wrong with us and turn that focus into worry and anxiety, we miss making the most of the moment we're in right now. We must ask ourselves these questions: *Where is my mind in this moment? Am I bitter toward anyone? Am I blaming my current mind-set on any person or situation? Is anger under the surface or right out in front of my demeanor today? Or am I peaceful? Kind? Loving? Focused on my most important people?*

How can we make this one single moment one we'll be proud of later? Well-lived moments equal a well-lived life. Yes, well-lived moments stacked upon well-lived moments accumulate into a well-lived life. I don't know if I heard that somewhere, or if I just know it to be true.

Well-lived moments stacked upon well-lived moments accumulate into a well-lived life.

We can work with only what's right in front of us—this moment here. There's no going back and changing, only forward movement. That's encouraging to me. My kids will best remember what's most recent to them.

What kind of memories will I give them starting right now?

39

Changing Our Tune

Anne-Renee

Goals today: Keep the tiny humans alive.

Anonymous

As a busy mom with a full calendar and a burning desire to follow hard after God, it seems almost comical to me how quickly I can move away from what I most want to pursue.

As we've been discovering, so many things can sideline and sidetrack us in responding to our Creator.

Selfishness is quick to creep in.

Busy schedules can engulf and overwhelm us.

Fears and worries, if allowed entrance, can shackle our minds, boisterously telling hypothetical stories and lies, while pushing everything else out, like truth and trust.

Competition is a sneaky ruler, especially when cleverly disguised, and it's quite adept at getting in the way of confidence and friendship.

Laziness, especially for the exhausted mom, likes to take over and *loves* to call the shots.

Then there's pride. And family drama. And the forgetting of grace.

The possible list of distractions is as endless and varied as our lifestyles, stories, and demographics. And when we're not fully fixed on

God, our focus moves elsewhere. Onto our stresses. Our struggles. Our strivings.

What distracts us begins to define us, guide us, and control us, steering us down paths we weren't meant to walk, blinding us to the needs of others and deafening our ears to the cries of those hurting around us.

In our self-serving state, we forgo serving others. We let go of investing in the lives of those God has put right in front of us. We forget about listening, loving, and laying down one's life.

It's uncomfortable at times, this Jesus way of living. The loving others better than yourself. The doing good, even when the recipient is hateful toward you. The extending of blessing in response to cursing. And the praying for those who abuse and manipulate. (See Luke 6 for the full list.) Seriously? Who wants to do that?

Instead we go for what's easier. Quicker. More comfortable. Less likely to rattle our souls or move us toward any kind of meaningful action. In response, we close our hands and our homes to those outside our tightly drawn circle, keeping our eyes fixed on us—our needs, our wants...our, our, our...

We become our own biggest distraction, the thing perpetually in the way of pursuing Christ. The roadblock to working toward a deepened relationship with Him.

But what can we do? We're just human, after all. Flawed creatures living in a sinful world.

I know I keep mentioning the importance of being in God's Word, but it really is a game changer. A perception shifter. A perspective manufacturer. It's the compelling voice of conviction when the waters of life seem murky and unknown. So in this writing process, I've been trying to closely monitor and evaluate how I spend my days, looking for patterns and pitfalls and generally whatever takes the bulk of my time and attention. And not too surprisingly, I keep coming back to the same time suck and same emotional drains.

My guess is you won't be too surprised, but for me, hands down, it's social media.

And all of us with our phones sitting within grabbing range cringe and whimper, "Please, no! Say it isn't so!"

Yup, it is.

Checking social media is the first thing I do when I arrive at the school pick-up lot. It's my go-to for doctor and dentist waiting rooms. It's the time filler for monotonous mom moments, like practices for sports, choir and band concerts, ballet recitals, and theater productions. It helps me through the weekend's wind-down and the next week's windup. It's my relaxation and my recreation. It's the gauge I use to assess my life, checking to see how I'm doing as a wife, mom, boss, and friend.

Social media has become my scale and lens for how I weigh life and perceive value, for good and for evil. But it leaves me wanting more—more stories, more entertainment, more pictures and quotes and comforting, soothing words. It cannot and will not feed truth to my soul the way God's Word can!

John Piper wrote,

> My feelings do not define truth. God's word defines truth. My feelings are echoes and responses to what my mind perceives. And sometimes—many times—my feelings are out of sync with the truth. When that happens— and it happens every day in some measure—I try not to bend the truth to justify my imperfect feelings, but rather, I plead with God: Purify my perceptions of your truth and transform my feelings so that they are in sync with the truth.[1]

Yes, sometimes what I find on social media nourishes and encourages me in my walk with the Lord. But most of the time, I must wade through the valley of the shadow of yuck before I get to that other side where the end of the rainbow is waiting with that tiny golden nugget of earth-shattering wisdom and truth. So it is with the greatest love for your and for my own soul, I say the following:

We need to spend less time sucking in what everyone else is doing on social media and spend more time soaking in the truth of God's Word. No more *Woe is me* and way more *Greater is He!* For "he who is in you is greater than he who is in the world" (1 John 4:4).

Something happens when we shift our focus, moving our eyes and our efforts from ourselves, and onto Him. Something daring. Something life-altering. Our faith becomes less of a label or badge to brag about and wear and more about *His* faithfulness. What *He* is doing in us and through us, for *His* glory. It's no longer just a dose of religion or role to play, but an intentional friendship with the Maker and Shaker of our souls. Our lives begin to be defined by the audacious, truth-speaking Spirit residing within us, breathing in us and through us. New life. New love. New meaning and purpose. And because of His love, because of His mercy, He compassionately moves us out of our self-satisfying state of complacency and into a living, breathing, real-deal walk of faith.

His transforming work within us not only changes us but changes our tune. We become willing to give of our time, influence, resources, wealth, and reputation—all for Christ. And because of the difference He has made in us, our hearts begin to stir. To be moved to action with a desire to share. To be generous out of the overflow. Suddenly we want to extend that love, that hope, and that grace to others.

It's heart-changing and it's life-changing.

With our eyes fixed on Him, we are set free from distractions, released and liberated to wholeheartedly pursue Jesus. And isn't that what life here on earth is all about? To share the good news? To live it out in the everyday, in the good seasons and the hard ones too?

40

Redeeming and Reclaiming

Anne-Renee

God doesn't want something from us; he simply wants us.

GERALD SITTSER[1]

How often do you think the disciples stressed out about insignificant details, forgetting in the heat of the moment what the moment was really all about?

As a believer in Jesus, I say I want to be His disciple. A follower. An apprentice. "Teach me, Lord," I pray as I dig into His Word and attempt to soak up its richness.

I proclaim loudly and repeatedly that I want to walk in His footsteps. But so often I feel like I'm failing the test, forgetting that my "times are in [His] hand" (Psalm 31:15). That what I think of as *my* work, *my* callings, and *my* day are really all *His* business. And, essentially, that this life I say I've given fully to Him, is far from surrendered.

Right before Jesus fed the five thousand, His disciples were urging Him to say goodbye to the crowds. Their solution to pushy people and groaning bellies was to send them away, directing them to the surrounding villages to buy their own sustenance. They didn't realize they already had the exact ingredients Jesus intended to use for a successful meal.

I mean, why would the people stay? It was a desolate place, the day was at its end, and everyone was hungry. Obviously, there was no purpose or reason for them to hang around, except to hear Jesus. Teaching and preaching might fill the mind and heart, but they couldn't fill an empty stomach. So the disciples came up with their own solution—a feasible, rational answer—all before even asking Jesus what He thought about the situation or what should happen next.

This was not the first time. The disciples were skillful at misunderstanding His methods. They argued over placement and rank. They questioned timing and protocol. And the parables He told? Those were super confusing! Then there was all that commotion over blessing the children. Were children welcome at His rallies? I mean, after all, Jesus was a busy man! What about His interaction and conversations with the outcasts of society? The prostitutes. The lepers. The lame. The blind. Folks a good Jew would have absolutely no dealings with normally. People like that adulterous, dirty rotten Samaritan woman. But there Jesus was, having a good ol' chat with her about her past husbands and living water.

The poor disciples. They weren't sure when to sleep or when to pray. And when was a good time to fight and cut off an ear, or simply listen to Jesus and be still. They were ordinary people following an extraordinary Messiah, but they were still unsure about how to even do that very well. They had spent all this time with the Savior of the world, but they still didn't understand the purpose behind the Suffering Servant, the fulfillment of the prophecies and His need to become the Lamb of God. Yet Jesus chose to surround Himself with folks like that, and oh, how that speaks hope into my heart.

How many times have I looked at what's in front of me and refused to see God's hand in it, when the miraculous seemed too hard to believe or too far beyond feasibility? Yet God, the Creator of all good things, loves to show us His power. His ability. His ever-expanding, limitless love. In the words of A.W. Tozer, "How completely satisfying to turn from our limitations to a God who has none."[2]

We've been doing an awful lot of talking about focusing on what really matters. And really, most of that can be boiled down to having an eternal outlook. The kind of perspective that sifts through the temporary and chooses the significant, giving clarity amid craziness, and purpose (as well as passion) to what He has placed right in front of us.

When our main focus as moms deepens into a desire to leave behind footprints of peace and hand down a legacy of love to our children (as well as those God puts in our path), our perspective begins to shift. Rather than allowing ourselves to be preoccupied by the dancing bees swarming around our heads, or all the shiny things surrounding us, we're choosing to fix our energies and eyes on what has eternal value: our faith, our families, and our callings.

Once again, it comes back to choice. Ann Voskamp says it like this, "Busy is a choice. Stress is a choice. Joy is a choice. You get to choose. Choose well."[3] We are daring to believe there's a different way to live. A life beyond distraction. I mean, seriously. What would happen if we flipped through the pages of Scripture as much as we flip through our social media feeds? What would that do to change the thermostat of our marriages, our families, our friendships? For God's Word changes everything, giving discernment, peace, joy, clarity, vision, wisdom, and so much more!

So as we close out this discussion on distracted mothering (at least for now), we want to challenge you not to walk away from this book unchanged. Take some time to jot down some of the things you've learned, the ways you've noticed distraction raising its ugly head in your day to day, and of course, ways you want to kick it to the curb. For our God is not a God of chaos. He is the Way, the Truth, and the Life. And He is waiting, just waiting, to spend time with you. Without all the noise, without all the interruptions, and without all the distractions.

Won't you join Him there?

Let's pursue wisdom and pursue peace. But ultimately, let's be moms who pursue Jesus. For *in Him*, "we live and move and have our being" (Acts 17:28).

A Prayer As We End

Father, we love You and we desire to honor You above all else. More than anything, we want to be women who proclaim and reflect You in our words and our actions, who bring You glory as we walk toward living a focused and intentional life for the sake of Your kingdom. Thank You for making us mothers. Thank You for trusting us with our children—these precious gifts. We humbly ask for Your help as we seek to keep our eyes fixed on You. Be our Strength and our Shield, we pray. In Jesus's name, amen.

All the Good Things

Beyond Shiny

To Remember

- We'll be remembered for who we are now more than who we've been in the past.
- Well-lived moments stacked upon well-lived moments accumulate into a well-lived life.
- We need less time sucking in what everyone else is doing on social media and more time soaking in the truth of God's Word.
- Sometimes *we* are our own biggest distraction—the thing perpetually in the way of pursuing Christ.
- We are set free from distractions when our eyes are fixed on the Lord.

To Hold On To:

My times are in your hand (Psalm 31:15).

In him we live and move and have our being (Acts 17:28).

Therefore, since we are surrounded by so great a cloud of witnesses, let us also lay aside every weight, and sin which clings so closely, and let us run with endurance the race that is set before us (Hebrews 12:1).

To Consider

Take a few minutes to read through *The Undistracted Mom Manifesto* on the following page.

We've loved walking with you through this book and hope you'll refer back to its message and this manifesto as often as you need. Because living the undistracted life is something we'll never regret.

The Undistracted Mom Manifesto

I, _____, desire to do my best in pursuing God and seeking His best for my family. I recognize the threat distraction poses in my life, and I want to choose the most important things. Today I will make faith a priority and make love my go-to response.

I commit to being a present, focused, and undistracted mom with an undivided heart.

I will work to identify the ways I'm distracted by all the shiny things.

I will resist the pull to be interrupted by what is not a priority, and I will choose to stay focused on what is a priority.

I will seek truth from God's Word, the Bible, and stop searching for acceptance and approval on social media.

I will refuse to get caught up in comparing myself with the women around me, and I will celebrate the incredible and brave moms I see.

I will do my best to concentrate on the people and callings God has put in front of me, even if that means turning off the TV, turning away from a good book, or putting my laptop across the room.

I will strive to put my phone down more often and look into the eyes of my people, because it matters to me, to them, and to the future of our family.

I purpose to live a life far from the lure of shiny things with a steady heart turned Godward in all I do, fixing my eyes on Jesus and all He has for me to do right now.

I resolve to love God and love my people well, giving them the best of my efforts and the bulk of my time.

Ultimately, I will aim to see God's unique framework for my life and fulfill my role in His story, for His glory.

And when I fail, which I'm bound to do, I will stand and try again, because living the undistracted life is worth it!

Signature:_____

Date:_____

A Note from the Authors

You can't go back and change the beginning, but you
can start where you are and change the ending.

Unknown

We made it.

The stories, experiences, and thoughts throughout this book hold our laughter and tears as well as our imperfect attempts to make the Word of God come alive for you, our dear reader. We appreciate the time you've dedicated to reading these pages, understanding that you could have been doing so many other things with the hours you've poured in here. Thank you for entrusting us with your time. Seriously. Just know that each word has been wrestled with, agonized over, and prayed through for you. Truly, this book is a labor of love from our laptops to your hands and hearts.

That said, we would love to hear what this book has stirred up in you. Maybe the distractions you're in the process of slaying or changes you'd like to make in the everyday. Tag us using the #shinythingsbook hashtag on social media or feel free to email us at info@themaster piecemom.com.

We would also like to invite you to become part of The Master-piece Mom community. We are a group of moms committed to praying for one another and dedicated to the art of embracing and spreading hope. Practically speaking, this means encouraging one another in the amazing task and gift of motherhood, however that looks, with unique roads and vastly different everyday lives. Yes, we are a spicy-fun combination of moms, desiring to love our families well and mother to the best of our abilities. Our goal is for each member to draw closer to the Lord in this community, and for every mom to know to the soles of her exhausted mama feet that she is not alone. We'd love for you to join us.

Thanks again for inviting us in. We're cheering for you!

From the two of us with love,

Amanda and Anne-Renee

The Masterpiece Mom—
www.TheMasterpieceMom.com

All the Mom Things Podcast—
www.allthemomthingspodcast.com

Instagram—
@amanda_bacon_
@anne_reneegumley

Facebook—
The Masterpiece Mom

www.amandabacon.com

www.anne-reneegumley.com

Notes

Chapter 1—Don't Blame It on the Shiny Things
1. *The Merchant of Venice* (1596), 2.7.69. References are to act, scene, and line.
2. Leslie D. Weatherhead, *Prescription for Anxiety* (London: Hodder & Stoughton, 1956), 31.
3. John C. Waugh, *One Man Great Enough* (San Diego, CA: Harcourt, 2007), 185-86.

Chapter 2—What It Costs
1. Rachel Macy Stafford, *Hands-Free Mama* (Grand Rapids, MI: Zondervan, 2013), 78.

Chapter 3—A Million Different Directions
1. Oscar Wilde, "Hélas," *Complete Works of Oscar Wilde* (London: Collins, 1966), 709.

Chapter 5—Rescuing Our Own Lives
1. Benjamin Franklin, *Poor Richard's Almanack and Other Writings,* ed. Bob Blaisdell (Mineola, NY: Dover Publications, Inc., 2013), 143.

Chapter 6—The Givers and Their Guilt
1. Emily P. Freeman, *Simply Tuesday* (Ada, MI: Revell, 2015), 95.

Chapter 7—It's All Good
1. Annie Dillard, *The Writing Life* (New York: Harper Perennial, 2013), 32.

Chapter 8—What Kind of Yes Is It, Anyway?
1. JJ Heller (@jjhellermusic), "Don't say yes because you're tired of saying no," Instagram, August 11, 2017, instagram.com/p/BXqdMlqAsG9/?hl=en&taken-by=jjhellermusic.
2. Lysa TerKeurst, *The Best Yes* (Nashville, TN: Thomas Nelson, 2014), 245.

Chapter 11—That Elusive Fine Line
1. Joshua Becker, "A Life Worth Waking Up For," *Becoming Minimalist*, 2015, https://www.becomingminimalist.com/wake-up/.
2. Mark Buchanan, *Spiritual Rhythm* (Grand Rapids, MI: Zondervan, 2010), 104.

Chapter 12—We're All Seeking Something
1.   Kristen Strong, *Girl Meets Change* (Ada, MI: Revell, 2015), 36.

Chapter 13—Too Busy for the Essentials
1.   Lewis Carroll, *Alice's Adventures in Wonderland & Through the Looking-Glass* (Ware, Hertfordshire: Wordsworth Editions Limited, 1993), 43.
2.   Greg McKeown, *Essentialism: The Disciplined Pursuit of Less* (New York: Crown Business, 2014), 123.

Chapter 14—Too Busy to Love
1.   Jane Austen, *Emma* (New York: Penguin Books, 1996), 249.
2.   Shane Freeman, "Ephesus," sermon, Southbrook Church, Weddington, NC, October 15, 2017, subsplash.com/southbrookchurch/media/mi/+zx9j4v9.

Chapter 15—Distracted by Everyone and Everything
1.   Bob Goff (@bobgoff), "We won't be distracted by comparison if we're captivated with purpose," Twitter, November 28, 2014, twitter.com/bobgoff/status/538346879474749441.
2.   Frederick Buechner.

Chapter 16—When Comparison Is a Good Thing
1.   George Müller, *The Autobiography of George Müller* (London: James Nisbet & Co., 1905), entry for May 7, 1841.

Chapter 17—Our Regular Life Is Just So Much
1.   Frances Hodgson Burnett, *A Little Princess* (New York: Puffin Books, 2014), 121.
2.   Elisabeth Elliot, *Let Me Be a Woman* (Carol Stream, IL: Tyndale, 1999 edition), 31.

Chapter 18—Untimely Desires
1.   Timothy Keller, *Prayer* (New York: Penguin Books, 2014), 228.

Chapter 19—What the Daydreams Won't Tell You
1.   Elisabeth Elliot, *Keep a Quiet Heart* (Ada, MI: Revell, 2004), 20.

Chapter 20—The Uncomfortable Wait
1.   Ben Patterson, *Waiting: Finding Hope When God Seems Silent* (Downers Grove, IL: InterVarsity Press, 1989), 11.

Chapter 21—Looking Up Long Enough to See
1.   TerKeurst, *The Best Yes*, 91.

Chapter 23—Living in a Pain-Shaped Reality

1. Nichole Nordeman, "Music, Motherhood, and Moxie with Nichole Nordeman," September 26, 2017, in *For the Love with Jen Hatmaker*, podcast, jenhatmaker.com/episode-07-nichole-nordeman.htm.

2. C.S. Lewis, *The Problem of Pain* (New York: HarperCollins, 2001), 92.

Chapter 24—You Don't Hear Me Saying *Yes, Please* to Stress

1. Ann Voskamp, *One Thousand Gifts* (Grand Rapids, MI: Zondervan, 2011), 159-60.

Chapter 26—Saying Welcome with Your Life

1. Kristen Welch, *Raising World Changers in a Changing World* (Grand Rapids, MI: Baker Books, 2018), 125.

2. Billy Graham, *The Journey: Living by Faith in an Uncertain World* (Nashville, TN: Thomas Nelson, 2007), 275.

Chapter 28—When I Pile My Plate with Worry

1. Elliot, *Keep a Quiet Heart*, 53.

2. Victor Hugo, *The Letters of Victor Hugo,* ed. Paul Meurice (Boston and New York: Houghton, Mifflin and Company, 1898), 23.

3. Robert Robinson, "Come, Thou Fount of Every Blessing," 1758.

4. Corrie ten Boom, *Each New Day: 365 Reflections to Strengthen Your Faith* (Grand Rapids, MI: Revell, 1977), May 29 entry.

Chapter 29—When We Want It to Be All Their Fault

1. Leo Tolstoy, *Anna Karenina*, trans. Richard Pevear and Larissa Volokhonsky (New York: Penguin Books, 2000), 683.

Chapter 30—Procrastinating Like It's My Job

1. Blaise Pascal, *Pensées*, trans. Honor Levi (Oxford: Oxford University Press, 1995), 10.

2. Brian Tracy, *Eat That Frog* (Oakland, CA: Berrett-Koehler Publishers, 2017).

Chapter 31—The Art of Avoidance

1. Anne Frank, *Tales from the Secret Annex,* trans. Susan Massotty (New York: Bantam Dell, 1982), 29.

Chapter 32—Contentment and the Plain-Jane Everyday

1. Jennifer Dukes Lee, *The Happiness Dare* (Carol Stream, IL: Tyndale Momentum, 2016), 127.

2. Jane Austen, *Pride and Prejudice* (London, England: Thomas Egerton, 1813).

3. Chrystal Evans Hurst, *She's Still There* (Grand Rapids, MI: Zondervan, 2017), 134.

Chapter 33—Who Am I When the Wi-Fi Goes Off?
1. Laura Ingalls Wilder, "A Bouquet of Wild Flowers" *The Missouri Ruralist*, July 20, 1917.
2. Michael Graham, "What Happens When a Hurricane Destroys Your Distractions," *The Gospel Coalition*, September 16, 2017, www.thegospelcoalition.org/article/when-a-hurricane-destroys-your-distractions/.

Chapter 34—The Regret of Lost Time
1. Every effort has been made to trace the source of this quotation.
2. *The New City Catechism: 52 Questions and Answers for Our Hearts and Minds*, The Gospel Coalition (Wheaton, IL: Crossway, 2017).

Chapter 36—Listing It Is Easier Than Living It
1. William C. Hannan, "The day will be what you make it," Instagram, October 16, 2014, instagram.com/p/uNy6UTqmlt/?taken-by=williamc.hannan.
2. Charlene Gubash and F. Brinley Bruton, "Egypt Mosque Attack Leaves at Least 305 Dead in Sinai Peninsula," NBC News, November 24, 2017, www.nbcnews.com/news/world/egypt-mosque-attack-leaves-dozens-dead-wounded-n823746.
3. Shannan Martin, *Falling Free* (Nashville, TN: Thomas Nelson, 2016), 203.

Chapter 37—Making Them Feel Differently
1. Leanna Tankersley, *Begin Again* (Grand Rapids, MI: Revell, 2018), 167.
2. Taffy Brodesser-Akner, "Tonya Harding Would Like Her Apology Now," *New York Times*, January 10, 2018, https://www.nytimes.com/2018/01/10/movies/tonya-harding-i-tonya-nancy-kerrigan-scandal.html

Chapter 39—Changing Our Tune
1. John Piper, *Finally Alive: What Happens When We Are Born Again* (Scotland: Christian Focus Publications, 2009), 165-66.

Chapter 40—Redeeming and Reclaiming
1. Gerald L. Sittser, *The Will of God as a Way of Life: Finding and Following the Will of God* (Grand Rapids, MI: Zondervan, 2000), 32.
2. A. W. Tozer, *Knowledge of the Holy: Drawing Closer to God Through His Attributes* (New York: HarperCollins, 1961), 47.
3. Ann Voskamp (@AnnVoskamp), "Busy is a choice. Stress is a choice. Joy is a choice. You get to choose. Choose well," Twitter, April 22, 2015, https://twitter.com/annvoskamp/status/590858264214171648.

Acknowledgments

From Both of Us

Thanks to...

Hope and Kathleen—who helped us refine this message and fueled our passion, and who believed this Masterpiece Mom thing was bigger than a book and more like ministry.

Emily P. Freeman—who believed in us before we were even sure we believed in ourselves and challenged us to cultivate the art within.

Our awesome Fedd Agency peeps—You gals are the reason moms can pick up this book and learn to set their distractions aside. Words cannot describe our thanks. And Whitney, quite simply, you're an all-star!

All our She Speaks friends and beloved Hope*writers family—You've been there from the very beginning, and we are so grateful for you. Janee, Andrea, Teri Lynne, Lisa-Jo, and the Chatters especially—thank you.

The whole team at Harvest House—thank you for taking a chance on us first-time authors and for being the kindest, most encouraging publishing house around.

From Amanda

Jeremy—I couldn't possibly list all the ways you've made this project a reality. Thank you for the grace and time you've extended to me. We make the best team, and I'm so thankful to be on this road with you. 143.

All the Bacon bits: Drew, Gavin, Morgan, Jackson, Annie, Gabi, Levi, and Emmy—your hugs and encouragement and how you let me sit and write in the middle of our chaos is the best! You guys make me smile.

My parents and family—*Dad and Marla Kay, Mom and Darrel, David and Anita Bacon*, what more could a girl say? It's not every day someone receives the gift of three amazing sets of parents. You have been cheering for me since the moment we met. Thank you. *Sean and Jen, the coolest big brother and sister*—some of these stories are your stories too. I love you.

Supportive friends Carly, Shannon, Jessica x 2, Shelley, Julie, and the dear people of WBC and Southbrook—your faithful friendship and love for our family moves me.

Amber—you have taught me what it means to sacrifice for a friend in need. I will always be grateful for you and the life you lived. I miss you like crazy. Heaven is brighter because you're there.

Lysa, Leah, Kimberly, and the whole gang at Proverbs 31 Ministries—working with and learning from you is one of my favorite parts of life.

The One who holds all things together, Jesus—my thanks will go on forever.

From Anne-Renee

Andrew—Thank you for supporting my crazy dreams despite my occasional forgetfulness in making dinner and all those late nights and weekends spent wrestling with words. You are my rock and my greatest love outside of Jesus. XOXOXXX…!

Kailee and Jamison—You are the best cheerleaders anyone could ever have. Thank you for sharing your hearts, your smiles, and laughter with me. I can't wait to see what God has up His sleeve for you two! If you hear a loud whistle, know it's your proud mama cheering from the sidelines.

My folks, Gary and Rebecca—You believed in my calling even before I was born, and have prayed me through the best and hardest of seasons. Your love and support means the world!

The numerous friends, family, and prayer warriors behind this project: Jane, Kristen, Alayna, Sarah, Andrea, Hal, Portia, Damion, Melots, Walkers, the Stewart clan, the Alaska fam, SE and SOT crew, the original MOPS gals, our P31 peeps, WBC family of faith, and the Vancouver, Washington Bible study friends who meet at Shirley's house—Your prayers and encouragement laid a firm foundation for this book. Couldn't have done it without you!

My Lord and Savior, Jesus Christ—You are my all in all.